LISA SCHADE ECKERT

How   n?

ENGAGING R   RARY THEORY

FO

LEILA C

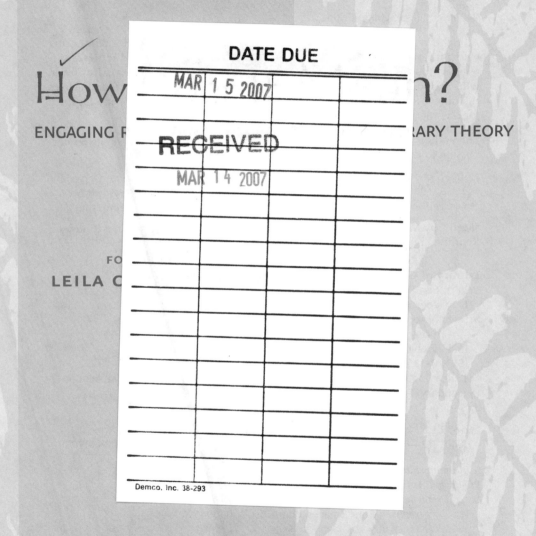

HEINEMANN
PORTSMOUTH, NH

Heinemann
A division of Reed Elsevier Inc.
361 Hanover Street
Portsmouth, NH 03801–3912
www.heinemann.com

Offices and agents throughout the world

© 2006 by Lisa Schade Eckert

The author and publisher wish to thank those who have generously given permission to reprint borrowed material:

"Fifteen" by William Stafford from *The Way It Is: New & Selected Poems.* Copyright © 1966, 1998 by the Estate of William Stafford. Reprinted from *The Way It Is: New & Selected Poems* with the permission of Graywolf Press, Saint Paul, Minnesota.

"Myth" by Muriel Rukeyser. Copyright © 1973 by the Estate of Muriel Rukeyser. Reprinted by permission of International Creative Management, Inc.

Library of Congress Cataloging-in-Publication Data
Eckert, Lisa Schade.
  How does it mean? : engaging reluctant readers through literary theory / Lisa Schade Eckert.
      p. cm.
  Includes bibliographical references and index.
  ISBN 0-325-00974-0 (alk. paper)
  1. Reading (Secondary)—United States.   2. Literature—Study and teaching (Secondary)—United States.   3. Literature—History and criticism—Theory, etc.—Study and teaching (Secondary).   I. Title.

LB1632.E27 2006
428.4071'2—dc22   2006009970

Acquisitions Editor: Lisa Luedeke
Production: Lynne Costa
Cover design: Jenny Jensen Greenleaf
Cover photograph: © Getty Images/PhotoDisc 21000047223
Typesetter: Kim Arney
Manufacturing: Steve Bernier

Printed in the United States of America on acid-free paper
10   09   08   07   06   VP   1   2   3   4   5

Contents

Foreword

A few years ago I returned to teach high school, and at the beginning of the semester I shared with my twenty-two eleventh graders what I expected of them. Teaching is, of course, a reciprocal act, so I also asked the students to share what they expected from me. To keep it honest, I gave the students cards on which they could anonymously write their comments, and I collected the cards and studied them carefully before we began our semester work together.

From the twenty-two I mostly received what a teacher would expect: the students wanted me to be flexible, be fun, and make the class interesting and challenging. A number of the comments, though, specifically addressed the study of literature, and my students touched on issues they felt were important enough to highlight.

What did the twenty-two students want regarding the teaching of literature? Some wanted more in-depth and compelling discussions, as the following excerpts from their cards reveal:

1. I would like to really get into great literature and discuss it all, not just the theme.
2. Present the literature in an exciting, interesting way.
3. I expect some in-depth detail of what we're reading in a discussion.
4. In reading I want to go in depth—I feel in high school we skim through novels some times that way I can't enjoy it.
5. I expect to be educated on literature.

But from three students, there were more pointed and, in some ways, more challenging comments:

6. Teach us how to analyze/interpret literature *properly.*
7. It'd be nice if while we're reading things, we could discuss hidden meanings and things like that.
8. All I really expect is that you give us direction, but don't limit us creatively or in our interpretation of the novels.

These three comments are pertinent to the work of Lisa Eckert and *How Does It Mean?*

First, how does a teacher help students interpret literature *properly*? How do we encourage students to see a multiplicity of analyses, all of which may well, in context, be proper and appropriate? Second, how do we invite students to look beyond what they often feel are the tricks of literature, the *hidden meanings*? How do we teach students who suspect that literature is really a game of smoke and mirrors, a series of esoteric codes and clues rather than an organic whole? Third, how do we use the structure of criticism in a positive, liberating way? How do we move students from a belief that *creativity* of interpretation is the sine qua non and that "it's my opinion, so it must be right" is the last, unassailable word in a discussion?

In their beginning-of-the-semester comments, my twenty-two students set before the class and me three difficult tasks. While we worked hard as we read short stories, poems, novels, and plays, the support of *How Does It Mean?* would have been helpful as I taught.

In *How Does It Mean?*, Lisa Eckert uses five approaches to critical theory to explode the notion of what is *proper* in interpretation, a comment that cannot entirely be dismissed as the province solely of a possibly naive high school junior. Many teachers as well fret that there is indeed a right interpretation to what we read and teach, and some, like my high school students, also worry that the hidden meanings and clues are essential prior to understanding. Neither is true, and in Chapter 1 of *How Does It Mean?*, Eckert contends that serious attention to literary theory can help students take ownership of their own interpretations and hold multiple, ever-contradictory interpretations simultaneously:

> Introducing different theoretical approaches into the literature class-room encourages students to consciously use everything they know to construct meaning from a text, and gain an understanding of what they are doing when they read and respond . . . Making literary theory an explicit part of instruction provides a teacher with opportunities to model ways of reading instead of merely translating a text. . . . Students learn ways of arguing the possibilities of multiple meanings and are empowered to take on the challenge of doing so.

This is the kind of approach we want for our students; specifically, using archetypal, objective, reader response, biographical and historical, and thematic approaches can enrich and deepen understanding. When these multiple approaches are explored, students are far less likely to believe that their own creativity is somehow limited by a teacher-presented interpretation. The lens is less a personal or egocentric one than one that has theoretical underpinnings and that can be used in a variety of ways. For Eckert,

> . . . there is also much to be valued in learning that texts don't just "happen," they are crafted . . . I wanted to teach objective theory, not merely enforce or defend close reading for the "right" meaning. Teaching such text-based strategies in relation to other interpretive methods as part of an overall repertoire of meaning-making strategies [that] can actually help students identify why they respond to text at all.

How Does It Mean? is a significant and accessible book; Eckert takes us into her classroom and, as she did in her award-winning 1996 article in *English Journal*, shows real-world appreciation of presenting theory to high school students—and making it work. As *EJ* editor many years ago, I was delighted to share with readers Eckert's approach; now, in *How Does It Mean?* it is broadened and deepened, guiding literature work in the high school classroom and giving students and teachers solid advice, real-world examples, and a thorough consideration of not just one, but multiple critical approaches.

It almost makes me want to go back and teach high school again—

—Leila Christenbury
Virginia Commonwealth University, Richmond

Acknowledgments

This book is a result of the encouragement from the many teachers I've had along the way. Teachers come in many forms: students who have taught me at least as much as I've taught them; colleagues who have encouraged and supported me throughout my career; members of my family who have patiently given me the inspiration, space, and time to work; and the institutions that provided the means to get the work done.

Specifically, I'd like to thank Janet Alsup, Karen McConnell, Jean Tittle, and Susan Talanda for being model English educators, supportive colleagues, and loyal friends. I would also like to thank Allen Webb and Constance Weaver for their inspiration and direction.

Thanks to Heinemann executive editor Lisa Luedeke for her vision, constant encouragement, and insightful editing to perfect the details. The Purdue Research Foundation and Purdue University College of Liberal Arts teaching and research incentives provided the necessary support to complete the manuscript. My thanks to them.

Most important, I send a heartfelt thank-you and much love to my family: to my brothers for inspiring me to "make it happen" and for refusing to allow me to succumb to the daily demands of a busy life; to my mom and my sons, who have made many sacrifices so I could teach, learn, and write; and to my husband, Greg, whose encouragement, support, and patience helped me see this book through to completion.

1 A Reason to Read: Why Literary Theory Engages Reluctant Readers

Everything we do in life is rooted in theory.
—bell hooks

"You look tired," a student in my British Literature class observed, as I stood taking attendance in the front of the classroom. On the day that I would later mark as the beginning of my epiphany about teaching and learning, I was tired. It was early spring in Michigan, which means it was damp and cloudy, and I was recovering from the process of having completed a paper for class that was due later that day. I was in my third year of teaching English at a suburban high school and taking a night class on literary theory. My students were often curious about what I was up to, with books and papers littered on and around my desk. After I shared the reason for my somewhat disheveled appearance, another student asked, "How can you write a whole paper on literary theory? What does that mean?" I started on a brief explanation, but as students asked more questions I found myself crudely diagramming different theoretical approaches on the chalkboard. Just as I heard myself say, "The question really isn't what does it mean, the question is how does it mean," the bell signaled the end of class. As they filed out the door, I stood rooted in front of my sketches, struck by the students' curiosity about the "secrets" of literary interpretation, the significance of wondering *how* instead of *what* words on the page mean to a reader, and how quickly the class period had passed. I had no way of knowing that these questions would lead to a fundamental change in my pedagogical and personal beliefs about teaching and learning. Nearly by accident, I stepped into the role of teacher-researcher when I was handed the opportunity (or maybe I should say challenge) to capitalize on the students' curiosity.

A few weeks later I was assigned to teach a new, yearlong World Literature class being offered the next fall. The class was conceived as a "general" option, with no prerequisites; a safety net primarily for seniors who needed that last English credit to graduate, but open to juniors who didn't want to take literature courses designed for college preparation and students who couldn't fit anything else into their schedules to meet state graduation requirements. In other words, I was going to be the clean-up crew for students who weren't, as one aptly put it, "into reading or writing." This meant that I couldn't take anything for granted; some students had previously taken American and/or British Literature courses, while others had barely completed a "basic English" class. Using a world literature textbook, limited sets of yellowing classroom novels, and suggested curricular guidelines pulled from a buried file, I would be responsible for teaching the essentials of the writing process and literary interpretation. As I looked over the rows of novels lined up neatly in the English department office, I realized that students who had previously taken literature courses had already read some of them, while other students, who had taken the general English courses, had probably never had the opportunity to read any of them, and it might very well be a struggle to get some students to read at all. Because they were coming from a wide span of socioeconomic and academic backgrounds, I was going to have to meet the needs and reading proficiencies of a very diverse group of learners. How could I best address the vast topic of world literature, differentiate instruction, and encourage them to develop the strategies to construct meaning from such a wide variety of texts? I felt overwhelmed as I contemplated how I would organize such a class, and realized that I didn't really know why I taught some of the things I taught. I knew it was my duty to be sure I covered basic literary conventions, the writing process, appropriate vocabulary, and all the basic state-mandated and suggested standards. But I wasn't sure how to decide what was most important, or how best to integrate comprehension instruction and encourage student engagement with text. So far, I had been teaching my students essentially in the same way I had been taught in high school, even though I faced a classroom full of people who lived in a world far removed from mine.

This was not the first time I struggled with the "how" of teaching English. One particularly vivid memory of this struggle is the time I had gone round and round with a freshman Introduction to Literature class on the first day of a unit on poetry. As I introduced the unit, students groaned.

"You're going to make us do a poetry notebook, aren't you?" one accused.

"We'll have to memorize one, won't we?" asked another. The class murmured unhappily, until one student announced "Poetry is stupid."

Stupid?

I stood there for a minute. How should I answer that? I patiently explained that poetry may be difficult at times, but was certainly not stupid. People had been writing poetry since the beginning of language itself, smart people who had something to say. Was I to understand that this suburban American class of fifteen-year-olds was pronouncing that some of the most moving words recorded in the history of humanity were *stupid*? I even pointed out that many of the songs they enjoyed listening to were forms of poetry. No luck. "We don't listen to the words," said one student, as if she couldn't believe I didn't know that.

They just looked at me, and another student repeated, for emphasis, "Poetry is stupid."

I was stunned. I took it personally. I tried again to reason with them until another student gave the Final Word: "My dad says I will never need poetry again in real life after I'm done with school." That was it. I devolved miserably to the "do it or else" method of motivation and delivered the classic ultimatum. "Well! If you want to pass this marking period, then you'll have to read some poetry." I even (and I'm so embarrassed to admit this) decreed that anyone who used the "s-word" ("stupid") in regard to poetry for the duration of the unit would lose five grade points immediately, starting with the first infraction. The very next day, a young man (who sat in the first row, right in front of me) attached a piece of paper to his shirt button that proclaimed, in bold capital letters, "I HATE POETRY."

It was going to be a long four weeks.

It occurred to me, as I contemplated teaching a full year of World Literature, that when students said poetry was stupid, they really meant poetry made them feel stupid. It was so much easier for them to pounce first, reducing poetry to the level of stupidity rather than waiting to feel they were reduced to stupidity when they tried to find meaning in a poem. I thought I tried everything in that freshman class, but I couldn't seem to help them engage. Something was missing, and not just with poetry. I had also put them through fourteen weeks of *Great Expectations*, beating the novel to death in my zeal to have students analyze character, describe the structure of chapters and subplots, find autobiographical references, understand the time period, recognize the symbolism, know what the words meant, *and* clearly tell me how they felt about all of that. In the process, I dampened any enthusiasm they had for the novel because we spent far too much time and effort trying to recognize every literary quality. No wonder they dreaded the thought of poetry. We survived the poetry unit that year, but it was less than satisfying. And here I was, over a year later, still wondering how I could open up the world of literature for students who had little inclination or time to include it in their lives.

Like many teachers in the early years of their career, I had focused primarily on the "content delivery" part of my job in the classroom, but as I worked to construct the new course that summer, I found myself examining my pedagogical beliefs with a much more critical eye. I knew

I needed some kind of instructional focus but wasn't excited about the usual thematic or chronological approaches suggested by the "Teacher's Edition" of the textbook. I needed to somehow externalize the ways engaged readers approached a text, modeling strategies for constructing meaning as I taught literature. I hoped to encourage students in World Literature to become engaged, inquisitive readers, help them learn to find meaning for themselves, and, above all, not repeat anything close to the experience I'd had with the freshman poetry unit. I thought about how curious and open to discussing theory the students in my class had been that day we talked about how meaning takes shape in the mind of a reader, and an idea began to form. Why couldn't I use literary theory to structure units, differentiate instruction, and bring intellectually engaging approaches to the high school classroom literary experience?

Actually, I had thought about teaching theory before. The British Literature students' curiosity and interest weren't so different from my own, but it wasn't until I was sitting in a sophomore English class in college that I first learned about theory. The professor for the course was tough, his lectures punctuated with a New York accent and the occasional stab of his finger in the air. Personal responses to a poem were not good enough, and I anxiously prepared for class hoping I could fall outside his radar. One day we were discussing John Donne's poetry and an unfortunate student commented on what she had "read into" a poem.

"Students of literature do not 'read into' a poem, they interpret a poem!" the professor thundered. "Freshmen in high school 'read into' poetry because they don't know any better. By now, you should know the difference!" He launched into a fifteen-minute lecture about literary criticism, explaining the rationale of approaching a text structurally, archetypically, and biographically. The structural approach, he explained, examined the structure and text of a poem as the only accurate way of gaining meaning. The text was the thing, not the author's background or what the author might have meant, not our personal experiences or responses. A biographical approach, on the other hand, focused on the poet or author's background and personal experience as a crucial key to understanding the work. The archetypal approach identified recurring patterns of imagery and symbol that were similar throughout literature and meant something to us subconsciously. These patterns reflected a deeper sense of universal human experience. The professor didn't advocate one approach over the other; he just explained some basic differences in interpreting a poem. When we explicated a poem, he emphasized, we should have a clear critical approach in mind in order to make sense of it. His issue wasn't with our work or desire to learn, and he didn't make us feel lazy or stupid. He just felt that we had been shortchanged in literature classes so far.

"I don't know why they don't teach you this stuff in high school," he said. "How can you read literature if you don't know this?" I was struck by the significance of his point; how could I even read if I didn't know this? I was thrilled to know I didn't have to just wander through my personal responses to a text, hoping to say something a teacher would like, or at least accept. There was logic to constructing meaning from text that could help me find the language for clearly expressing what I thought. Why hadn't I ever learned about this before?

But now I was the teacher, and wanted to help my students read and connect with literature; the professor's words surfaced again, and I remembered what they had meant to me. Why couldn't I follow his example, and offer my own students the language and theoretical concepts to help them think critically and become cognizant of their own reading processes? Why couldn't I adapt these concepts to teach in the high school? It occurred to me that understanding the underlying approaches to constructing meaning from text didn't only apply to college (or college preparatory) literature classes; understanding how to assume a critical stance would help any student read any text. I decided to see what would happen if I used literary and critical theory to organize the way we approached the expanse of world literature. I wanted to discover how students would respond to theory, and if using theory *did* encourage awareness of how they constructed meaning from text, but also how theory is best introduced in a secondary English classroom. I searched for appropriate or even adaptable teaching materials or guides, but couldn't find any that suited the needs of my students. So I began to develop my own methods for using literary theory to organize the way I taught literature.

Choosing Theory, Designing Practice

There are, of course, more theories of literary interpretation in the field than I could possibly address in one class. Literary theory is, by nature, recursive, resulting in "a kind of cannibalization going on among Marxism, psychoanalysis, structuralism, poststructuralism, and so on. . . . The offshoot is a magma of interpretive discourses" (Iser 2000, 3). I needed to wade through the vast range of theory and identify some specific concepts to share with students. I referred to my dog-eared copy of M. H. Abrams' *A Glossary of Literary Terms* (1988) and a general theory text, settling on five general concepts: archetypal (or Jungian), objective, reader-response, genetic (biographical and historic), and thematic (ideological and philosophical). Then I sat down with the course materials I had in hand and matched up poetry, short stories, and novels to specific theoretical approaches that seemed to fit with the structure, content, or genre of each piece, leaving wiggle room for students to choose some of their own reading material. My intention was to use literary theory to scaffold student response, to give students the language for expressing their responses to what they read.

As I developed these lessons and units, I realized that including explicit instruction of theory in a literature classroom made perfect sense and just seemed so obvious, for lack of a better term. Including theory seemed to supply the "missing link" for setting specific goals and maintaining a sense of continuity for the different thematic or geographical areas we would cover. After all, I reasoned, hadn't most students already engaged in some theoretical methods of constructing meaning for a long time without knowing the "label" of the approach? How many times in the past had their English teachers covered basic plot structures of exposition, complication, climax, falling action, resolution? I was willing to bet that many teachers had already taught these very students to build an interpretation based on how a story is put together; how the exposition functions to first grab, then hold on to their interest, how the climax is intensely moving, the resolution satisfies by tying up loose ends. Why shouldn't they know they were using a structural approach? If they studied the American colonial period or read a poem set in World War II, why shouldn't they know they were using a sociohistoric or biographical approach? Providing labels for these methods would allow them to be privy to this "insider" information and help them to recognize they were learning an approach to the reading task, establishing essential prior knowledge and a strategy for constructing a meaning that could be defined, argued, and supported as the best or most appropriate. So I worked on, sketching out goals for the next year and hoping for the best. Because World Literature was a yearlong course, the units of study I include in this book span roughly twenty-five weeks (I don't include everything we covered, only those units in which I introduced a theoretical concept).

The first day of school arrived, and I was as ready as I would ever be. My new World Literature students strutted through the door, glanced at the textbook, and scoffed, "Yeah, here we go. More reading." Tom sprawled into a seat, exuding the confidence of a high school senior in his jaunty fisherman's cap, and said to his neighbor "You just BS about anything. We've done this already." He winked then looked at me. "Who decides this stuff is great, anyway?" Others chuckled at Tom's bravado as they sat down. Eyeing them as they settled, I took a deep breath and wrote two sentences on the board:

"WHAT does it mean?"
"HOW does it mean?"

They hesitantly began to puzzle through the questions. "What does that mean? What's the difference? Is that even good grammar? It doesn't make sense!" After I introduced myself, I asked them about the difference between the two questions. The first one was deceptively easy, but the second?

"I can tell you what I think something means to me," I explained. "The editors of the textbook can tell you what they think. But *how* do we come up with that meaning? How do we know if that meaning is right?" Students were dubious; they waited for me to answer the questions for them, but I bit my tongue. Finally one student responded, "You just think too much about what you read."

Teaching Theory, Teaching Reading

As I thought about that student's comment later, I was suddenly hit with a crucial insight (a friend of mine would call this a "cosmic two-by-four"): "teaching literature" is in many ways synonymous with "teaching reading." This may seem obvious, but I never thought of myself as a reading teacher. This is so significant to the rest of my story that I feel it necessary to elaborate for a moment on the implications of how students are taught to construct meaning from text at any grade level.

Consider the following conclusions drawn by leading scholars in the fields of reading and literary theory. Reading researcher Frank Smith asserts that "children cannot be taught to read. A teacher's responsibility is not to teach children to read but to make it possible for them to learn to read" (1997, 5). Literary critic Northrop Frye puts it like this:

> [it is] impossible to "learn literature": one learns about it in a certain way, but what one learns, transitively, is the criticism of literature . . .
> the difficulty often felt in "teaching literature" arises from the fact that it cannot be done: the criticism of literature is all that can be directly taught. (2001, 1446)

Both theorists lay the burden of teaching meaning construction on the ingenuity of the teacher, and both argue for explicit instruction of the underlying strategy rather than the words on the page. Theory is always present in an English classroom, just like reading is always present in an elementary language arts classroom. But, unlike their elementary counterparts who often plaster the classroom walls with reading strategies and engage in practices explicitly teaching them to students, secondary teachers rarely acknowledge using a specific theoretical perspective. Without this explicit instruction, students often don't understand what a teacher is asking for when she directs them to infer, interpret, or respond to literature. Gerald Graff clearly makes this point when he describes his early experiences with literature as

> being alone with texts . . . bored and helpless, since I had no language with which to make them mine. On the one hand, I was being asked to speak a foreign language—literary criticism—while on the other hand, I was being protected from that language, presumably for my own safety. . . . teachers cannot avoid translating the literature they teach into some critical language or other, [and] neither can students, for criticism is the language students are expected to speak and are punished for not speaking well. (2000, 45–47)

Kathleen McCormick also makes this point, arguing that "if students are to become active makers of meaning of texts, they must also be given access to discourses that can help them experience their own readings of texts" (1996, 305).

Teaching students to use literary theory as a strategy to construct meaning is teaching reading. Learning theory gives them a purpose in approaching a reading task, helps them make and test predictions as they read, and provides a framework for student response and awareness of their stance in approaching a text. They find new reasons to look closely at any given text (including those in popular culture) and added incentive to read, practicing "literate behaviors [that] are only engendered in situations that move beyond skill-building to provide opportunities to make and judge meanings" (Wilhelm 1997, 153). Even the most advanced students are still honing their literacy skills. These are the same cognitive processes they practiced in elementary school, but are often far removed from the secondary classroom.

Introducing different theoretical approaches into the literature classroom encourages students to consciously use everything they know to construct meaning from a text, and gain an understanding of what they are doing when they read and respond. They discover how they are constantly interpreting signals whenever they read, even though they may not be aware of doing so. They can develop an awareness of the meaning-making strategies they already employ or can learn to employ for improved comprehension and appreciation of text. Making literary theory an explicit part of instruction provides a teacher with opportunities to model ways of reading instead of merely translating a text. In my view, using theory as an instructional practice to differentiate reading strategy instruction is one of the most important things I learned as I taught World Literature.

As students become more aware of the strategies they use for constructing meaning from text, they can begin to recognize and question the ideological influences at work in a text. The influence of their own values and beliefs, as well as those inherent in a theoretical approach, come under scrutiny as they decide whether they accepted a certain set of principles and ideals regarding the meaning of a text. Students can question why a magazine advertisement or television commercial elicits an emotional response from them. They can scrutinize that response, and the ideological criteria they have unconsciously established, to evaluate such advertisements positively or negatively. A theoretical stance becomes an argument, a "reflective struggle" in which the "demand for proof and further defense . . . introduce[s] students to the rough-and-tumble of critical argument, the open-endedness of genuine inquiry" (Myers 1994, 332). Students learn ways of arguing the possibilities of multiple meanings and are empowered to take on the challenge of doing so. The argument is not with the teacher, however; it's centered on the theoretical approach and the reading itself. Each student must articulate his views in order to debate them with someone else. In fact, learning how to effectively argue for a particular interpretation is ideally suited for adolescent learners, whose behavior is often oppositional anyway. Constructing an argument is "more than simply a good reading strategy—it is also an essential survival tactic for overcoming the adversities that adolescents place before secondary teachers through their oppositional language and behavior" (Philion 2001, 56). Constructive argument is an important skill, not only for literary interpretation, but also to help them process many of the texts thrown at them by the world at large. A basic understanding of various theoretical approaches to text helps students become more effective readers in any reading situation.

Even though the students in the World Literature class began their literary scholarship reluctantly, in the long run they not only appreciated knowing different literary approaches, but became more skilled, critical readers and interpreters of texts. They experimented with and puzzled through theory, discussing what they had read with an understanding they hadn't experienced before. They assumed more responsibility for their interpretations; I didn't have to scrounge for quiz questions or essay topics which would only challenge their (and my) short-term memories. Instead, we could focus on the bigger picture of meaning and perspective. And they loved, loved, arguing with me and each other about the merits of one approach over the other. By the end of the year, it was apparent that teaching and applying specific critical approaches had succeeded beyond my most optimistic expectations. The students in World Literature taught me to have faith in their inherent need to make sense of the world around them, and recognize their right to discover that there is not always a right or wrong way of trying to do just that.

The Organization of this Book

Each chapter of this book presents the highlights of a specific unit I taught on theory, including a review of the essential concepts and theorists followed by examples of teacher modeling activities, discussion, handouts, assignments, and readings that we completed. I also offer some added suggestions for teaching theory as well as additional readings that a teacher may find useful or thought-provoking. There are, of course, countless texts that could be used in place of those I used and the instructional materials I include throughout this book can be adapted to any curricular goals. The methods I share in this book worked for me because they were mine; I designed and continually adapted them for my particular class and students. My hope is that teachers will be inspired to use them as a starting point and adapt them for their own students and curricular goals.

Further Teaching Suggestions

- Have students keep a Critical Notebook to continually reference throughout the duration of the class. This could be a three-ring binder to hold theoretical background information, poetry, short stories, their writing, assignments, and so on.

- After working with a particular theoretical approach, have students list three strengths and three weaknesses about using it as a means to construct meaning from a text. This serves to review and assess their understanding of the concept.

- Use the same short piece to model various theoretical approaches (rereading is a great strategy to model anyway). I used "Why Reeds Are Hollow" by Gabriela Mistral. Then students can focus on the approach rather than understanding a new story each time.

- Locate and photocopy brief excerpts from theoretical essays (I used *Contemporary Literary Criticism*, a reference work common to most libraries) or book reviews that assume different theoretical stances toward a text. Have students read them and decide which approach the author seems to be assuming and explain why they think so; whether they're right or wrong isn't as important as how they construct an argument. This can serve as review or assessment at the end of a unit as well as the beginning of discussion for a new unit on interpretation.

- Every unit of study doesn't dictate beginning a new theoretical approach. In this book, I've included only those units in which I did introduce a new approach; in others (Asian literature, for example), we just reviewed and applied approaches we had already covered. It was useful to save some units for additional practice to ensure student comprehension and keep our study of theory fresh.

- After students have learned two or three theoretical approaches, introduce a short story or poem and break the students up into small groups. Assign each group a theoretical method and have them read and determine a final meaning for the story or poem using the approach. Then bring the class back together to discuss and debate their understandings of the piece, focusing on how each group came to a conclusion based on their particular stance.

- Include readings from other media (websites, newspaper articles, etc.) and children's literature in applying theoretical approaches. Although interpretive expectations can be similar, the texts themselves can be less challenging and more accessible for English language learners and those who may struggle with reading and/or learning disabilities.

- Above all, don't worry about knowing everything there is to know about criticism and theory. Students were very open to learning with me some of the time rather than from me all the time.

Additional Readings

Culler, Jonathan. 2000. *Literary Theory: A Very Short Introduction*. New York: Oxford University Press, USA.

Eagleton, Terry. 1996. *Literary Theory: An Introduction*. Minneapolis: University of Minnesota Press.

Purdue University Critical Theory website: www.cla.purdue.edu/english/theory.

Ryan, Michael. 1999. *Literary Theory: A Practical Introduction*. Malden, MA: Blackwell Publishers.

Voice of the Shuttle website: http://vos.ucsb.edu.

2 Beginning at the Beginning: Teaching Myths and Archetypal Theory

Creativeness, like the freedom of the will, contains a secret.
                                            —C. G. Jung

Before launching into the archetypal theory unit, I needed to help students get their minds around the concept of literary theory in general. Even after spending the summer reading and planning, I was still a little nervous; I was afraid their eyes would glaze over or a full-class rebellion would break out. I took a deep breath, faced the class when the bell rang, and began.

"Yesterday we talked about the 'secrets' of understanding literature," I announced. "I think it's really about the 'secrets' of understanding anything we read. How do we understand what those black marks on a page, called letters, mean? What are you actually doing when you read?"

"Sleeping," smirked Tom, to the general amusement of the class. I didn't take exception to his answer. "Actually, this really is a hard question; no one really knows the answer. That's why there are different theories about how we actually construct meaning from those words on the page. So, Tom, what is a theory, anyway?"

"I guess the opposite of fact. It's something you try to prove," he answered.

"Right, it's like an idea or a guess based on observation. So different people who have spent a lot of time trying to figure out how we make words on a page mean something have different ideas. But how could they prove their idea is true?" The question was met with silence, except for the sound of shifting seats as students averted their eyes to avoid mine.

I tried again. "Yesterday someone said I think too much about what I read. Maybe that's true. Maybe I should think more about how I read instead. So, that's what we're going to do in this class. And guess what this kind of inquiry is called? [Dramatic pause for effect, which had none whatsoever.] Literary theory, because there are different theories about the ways we make sense of the words that make up everything we read."
I looked around for some kind of confirmation, interest, even a raised

eyebrow. They looked back blankly. "Well, there we are then," I said brightly, or lamely, depending on how I thought about it later. There was nothing to do but move on, so I started right into the first unit of study, archetypal theory.

Essentials of Archetypal Theory and Carl Jung

Noted literary critic Northrop Frye once wrote that in order to fully comprehend any text, the reader must crack the symbolic code embedded within; we are used to this notion already in various areas of our lives. To understand a sporting event, the crowd must crack the code of rules, behavior, and (the most difficult for me) referee signals and penalties. Understanding the coach's signals in baseball or playing a strict round of golf requires knowledge of elaborate symbolic codes. So do passing chemistry and algebra, attending a church service, and driving a car. Approaching a written work archetypically not only requires cracking a symbolic literary code, but also determining how that code creates meaning, stirring our deepest aesthetic appreciation for the work itself. There are two steps to understanding archetypes and then using them as a method of interpreting literature. First, students must understand the meaning of the term *archetype* and learn to recognize archetypal images, patterns, and characters in literature; second, they must understand the underlying significance of these patterns, using them to create meaning from a work. This is an intertextual approach to constructing meaning; a reader can explore the relationship and similarities between various texts instead of focusing only on the text at hand.

Early-twentieth-century psychologist Carl Jung coined the term *archetype* from the Greek word *archetypon*, meaning "beginning pattern." He described them as "identical psychic structures common to all" (Read, Fordham, and Adler 1953–78, V, para. 224), which constitute "the archaic heritage of humanity" (V, para. 259). According to Jung, these structures reside in every individual's psyche, regardless of race, nationality, or literary experience, controlling behavior and giving rise to similar thoughts, feelings, and images (Stevens 1994, 32–33). The exploration and evaluation of archetypes as a critical tool in literature is part of a much larger field of study led by Jung, who began his career as a disciple of Sigmund Freud. While the two psychologists agreed on the idea of the unconscious as a powerful force within the human mind, they disagreed on the role the subconscious mind plays in the human psyche of man. Freud understood the subconscious as a reservoir of repressed memories, desires, and fears, but Jung conceived of a deeper realm of being which communicates with consciousness in certain universally characteristic ways. In other words, Jung believed that within our subconscious mind we harbor our entire archetypal endowment in what he called the *collective unconscious*. The collective unconscious is a universal, shared consciousness that connects all human beings through inherent impulses, drives, and values; a "psychic system of a collective, universal and impersonal nature which is identical in all individuals. . . . [and that] does not develop individually but is inherited" (Stevens 1994, 33). This realm of the consciousness is inaccessible to the conscious mind; we cannot recall the experiences that reside there because, individually, we did not experience them. They are the experiences, or ideals, that have piled up over the generations and are stored in the subconscious mind. We are only aware of the power center of the collective unconscious: the *self*.

According to Jung, the self, or psyche, is the consciousness that an individual can recognize. The self includes three primary aspects: the *ego*, the *shadow*, and the *anima* (feminine) or *animus* (masculine). The ego represents that small portion of the mind that we recognize as thought, maturity, and reason. In the realm of the ego, we identify who we are, what we think and believe about the world and our place in it. The shadow, much like the Freudian id, is the dark side of the self, the hiding place for repressed desires, instinctive drives, and negative emotions. The anima or animus is the part of the self that harbors characteristics of the opposite sex; a man has an anima and a woman an animus lurking in the depths of their self. Jung argued that the goal of the individual is to achieve balance or recognition of the different aspects of self, and called this the process of *individuation* or *self-actualization*. To reach individuation, one must recognize, confront, and assimilate the ego, anima(us), and shadow into the larger realm of the self, achieving a new level of consciousness. Instead of being aware only of the ego personality, an individual becomes conscious of the vast reaches of the self. "The meaning of 'whole' or 'wholeness' is to make holy or to heal. . . . It is the way to the total being, to the treasure which suffering mankind is forever seeking"(Jung 1976, 123). Glenna Davis Sloan, in *The Child as Critic*, agrees, saying "literature is a continuous quest to rediscover a lost perfection, a truly human identity" (1991, 80). This "lost perfection" can be understood as the search for a return to a mythic time when "truth" could be known. The archetypes of self represent concepts that we, as individuals, cannot easily comprehend, and we realize the experience of wholeness repeatedly only through metaphor. Consequently, for most of us, self-actualization comes only in epiphanic flashes of insight or self-knowledge. These instances, however fleeting, can be intensely meaningful and transforming.

According to Jung, the individual's desire to know the self and reach into the depths of consciousness is the basis for all storytelling as we instinctively try to understand this deeper nature through metaphor.

Archetypes are repetitive images and metaphors that appear throughout mythology and literary works. Through continual storytelling, each generation expands upon the thoughts and knowledge of the preceding ones, but the core symbolic terms representing concepts that cannot be defined or fully comprehended remain much unchanged; they are produced by the human psyche unconsciously and spontaneously. Therefore, we instinctively respond to these images when we see or hear them in a story. Terry Eagleton puts it this way:

> when we evaluate [literature] we are speaking of ourselves. . . . The modes and myths of literature are transhistorical, collapsing history to sameness or a set of variations on the same themes . . . an expression of those fundamental human desires which have given rise to civilization itself. [Meaning] is not to be seen as the self-expression of individual authors, who are no more than functions of this universal system: it springs from the collective subject of the human race itself, which is how it comes to embody 'archetypes' or figures of universal significance. (1996, 80–81)

Teaching Archetypal Theory

I had taught mythology before, but even though students seemed interested in reading the old myths and legends, the subject seemed to lack substance. Students had usually read or listened to myths, legends, and folktales for years in school and felt it was just more of the same when they arrived in my class. But these ancient stories are all about archetypal patterns, and the combination of familiar stories (or story types) as a means for introducing unfamiliar concepts, like literary theory, made sense to me. I hoped to use archetypal theory to enhance the study of mythology by giving it a higher purpose (no pun intended), helping students find the means to say something about the myths and stories we read. But instead of detailing archetypal or Jungian theory right away (an overwhelming prospect for any students), I set smaller goals and prepared activities to ease them into the subject. I gradually introduced more complex concepts along the way, and the pieces of archetypal theory eventually fell into place. Adding archetypal theory didn't take much time; the entire unit as described here encompassed the first six weeks of school.

First, I defined the term *archetype* by asking students to think about myths or folktales they remembered from childhood and help me brainstorm a list of stories, events, and cast of characters. As they called out favorites like "Beauty and the Beast" and "Little Red Riding Hood," legendary figures including Hercules and King Arthur, mythological characters such as coyotes and dragons, I recorded what they said on an overhead transparency. When the transparency was full, I asked them to tell me what these stories, characters, events, and images had in common. They volunteered that there was always a heroic central figure, and I circled these with a blue transparency marker. They noticed the evil characters, and I circled these in green. They noticed that there was always a task, and I circled those in orange. Then I congratulated them for already knowing what an archetype is: a common pattern repeated over and over again in stories (which includes stories in movies, TV shows, and video games). "We're going to spend some time thinking about why there are so many commonalities in stories, and how these help us to find meaning in lots of things we read and see. Archetypes are not just found in myths, and I'm wondering if knowing about archetypes can help us understand other kinds of writing. If these stories are all so similar, why do we like them so much?"

I gave them a handout with a brief definition of archetypal theory, including three general categories of archetypes (images, character types, and plot structures) and a list of twenty-one common archetypes (Figure 2–1). I asked students to form small groups and sort each of the listed archetypes into the category they thought was most appropriate, then to discuss/answer the thought questions at the end. My goal was to further activate prior knowledge and generate some informal discussion about recurring patterns in literature, not to tell them exactly how each of the archetypes should be sorted. They had to think a little when they sorted the archetypes and talked generally in their groups about different manifestations of some of them, but found it easy to finish. After a few minutes we reconvened as a class and talked about how they had decided where to put each one. Some of the rituals they shared were holiday celebrations, graduations, birthdays, sporting events, weddings, and funerals. We didn't spend too much time on this, I just asked them to consider what purpose these rituals served and how they helped us define ourselves. I was hoping to make a basic connection between archetypal character, event, or image and the concept of personal identity in preparation for what would come next. I required students to keep the study guide as a reference throughout the unit, so if they ran into trouble identifying archetypes later they could refer to it for clues.

Primary and Secondary Archetypes

The real work came as I introduced Jung and his concept of self. "Remember those rituals we talked about? And how they helped us to define who we are? Those patterns in stories are kind of like that; they mean something to us whether we consciously think about it or not. An archetypal critic would say they mean something bigger, mirroring concepts that reside deep in the reader's consciousness. To read anything

Archetypal Criticism

This method of literary criticism (also known as "Jungian Criticism") identifies common patterns in literature that appeal to the reader's subconscious drives and uses them as a basis for discussion and interpretation of the meaning of a literary work. The term *archetype*, coined by noted psychologist Carl Jung, literally means "ancient/primitive pattern." A writer, poet, or artist serves as a kind of "spokesman" for the rest of us, recognizing our need to understand who we are, where we come from and where we are going, and what is important to us. The writer, consciously or unconsciously, uses archetypes to help us relate to a story or character and therefore to understand ourselves.

Some common categories of archetypes are:

objects or images
character types
patterns of events or plot designs

These are identifiable in a wide variety of works of literature as well as in myths, dreams, and even the social behavior and rituals in which we take part. When these patterns are successfully used in a work of literature, the archetypal critic says they evoke a profound response from the reader, who finds meaning in and enjoys the book, story, or poem.

Identification Exercise: From the following list of common *secondary* archetypes, decide which is an *object* or *image*, a *character type*, or a *pattern of events*. Write the number next to the appropriate heading above.

1. Death and rebirth	8. Evil monster	15. Tree
2. Trickster	9. Descent into abyss	16. Bird
3. The heroic quest	10. Water	17. Garden
4. Earth mother	11. Forest	18. Ritual bathing
5. Climbing mountains	12. Creation	19. Changing clothes
6. Rivers	13. Hero (protagonist)	20. Journey
7. Fatal woman/man	14. Anti-hero (antagonist)	21. Brother/sister

Thinking About Archetypes

1. Choose two of the archetypes from the preceding list. Cite a time in your life or in your reading when you have experienced this event, character, or image. Describe the experience and explain how it was significant either in your life or in the story you were reading.
2. List some "rituals" of social behavior you have experienced or will experience. Why do we engage in these rituals? What significance do they have on our lives? Are these "archetypal" behaviors or patterns of behavior that help us to define ourselves?

Figure 2–1   Archetypal Criticism

from an archetypal approach means looking for archetypes and considering how they make us think about our identity, or concept of self," I explained. I gave a brief overview of the Jungian self by giving them the "The Jungian Self" handout (Figure 2–2a) and projecting an overhead transparency of a blank "Jungian Self Diagram" (Figure 2–2b). I asked students to follow along as I explained each term, taking the definitions directly from the handout and labeling the diagram as I talked. This was all in preparation to help students distinguish between what I called primary archetypes and secondary archetypes. I explained that the ego, the shadow, the anima(us), and the collective unconscious were the primary archetypes of self, and these were represented by the secondary archetypes we had categorized into character, plot, and image. If students understood the concept of primary self archetypes, they could recognize the underlying meaning of secondary archetypes as manifestations of that self, and begin to understand how they help us to connect personally with a story. "For example, the primary archetype of the ego can be represented in a story as the secondary archetype of hero or protagonist; that of the anima as a beautiful maiden or horrifying monster; that of the shadow as nameless evil or a close friend; and that of the collective unconscious as a god or being who offers assistance or direction to the hero. These basic characters and elements of plot represent the different aspects of the self."

Next, students needed to connect the various archetypal images listed in the Archetypal Criticism handout (Figure 2–1) we had completed earlier to Jung's conception of the self: the ego, the shadow, and the anima or animus. I asked them to refer to the list of secondary archetypes and sort them again into the blanks on the student handout entitled Jungian Self Diagram (Figure 2–2b). The diagram has the correct number of blank spaces for secondary archetypes to guide classification. For example, the shadow has three blanks, one for antagonist, one for trickster, and one for evil monster (Good vs. Evil). The ego has only one blank, for the hero. I've included two versions of the diagram: the one I gave the students with only the numbered blanks (Figure 2–2b) and one that has the secondary archetypes filled in (Figure 2–2c). We discussed and completed this together in class. I started with the list of secondary archetypes because I thought they would be more familiar to students and less intimidating. Because they already knew some heroes, tricksters, and quests, it was easier to make symbolic sense of the ego, anima(us), and shadow. The handout and diagram also meant less time lecturing, and I really didn't want to start the project of understanding theory with a long, complicated lecture. Certainly the primary archetypes of the Jungian self could be taught first to accomplish the same end: having students actively

---

The Jungian Self
Important Terms and Concepts

The following terms 1 through 5 are the *primary* archetypes of self: the entire consciousness of an individual. Just as all colors of the rainbow stem from the primary colors, so do secondary archetypes of image, character, and plot stem from the primary elements of the reader's interaction with a story. These patterns are instinctively interpreted by readers, who have an emotional response and find meaning in what they read.

1. **Collective Unconscious:** Resides deep within the unconscious mind; to recognize this is to achieve the ultimate experience (enlightenment, nirvana, etc.), to become self-actualized

2. **Ego:** The conscious mind; who we believe we are

3. **Anima:** Feminine impulses within the male subconscious

4. **Animus:** Male impulses within the female subconscious

5. **Shadow:** The opposite of the ego; the negative or dark side

Some additional important terms relating to Jung's concept of self:

1. **Persona:** The image the ego projects to others

2. **Individuation:** The final goal of complete self-knowledge

3. **Transformation:** Changes the ego must undergo on the way to individuation

Figure 2–2b on page 20 (to be given to the students) represents an individual's self. The primary archetypes are indicated in bold; how many secondary archetypes (listed on the Archetypal Criticism worksheet) can you place with the appropriate primary archetype? The numbers in each area provide you with clues to how many secondary archetypes should be matched with each primary one.

Figure 2–2a   The Jungian Self: Important Terms and Concepts

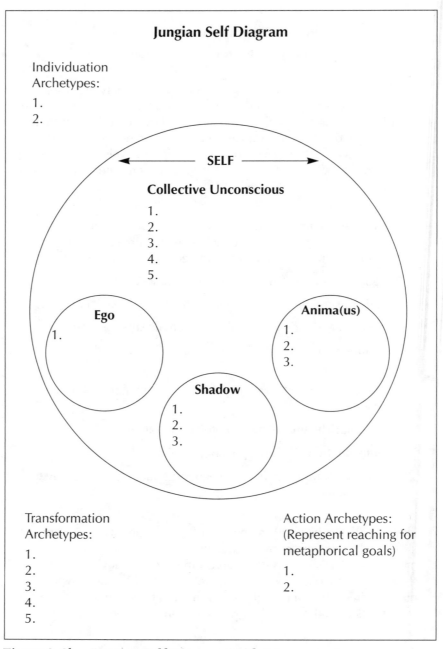

Figure 2–2b   Jungian Self Diagram (without answers)

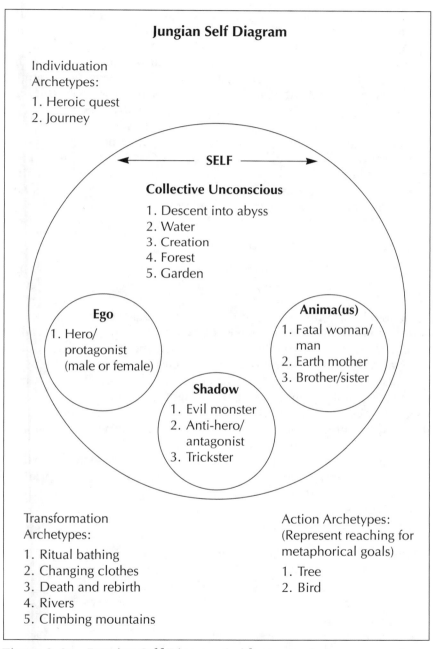

Jungian Self Diagram

Individuation
Archetypes:
1. Heroic quest
2. Journey

← SELF →

Collective Unconscious
1. Descent into abyss
2. Water
3. Creation
4. Forest
5. Garden

Ego
1. Hero/
protagonist
(male or female)

Anima(us)
1. Fatal woman/
man
2. Earth mother
3. Brother/sister

Shadow
1. Evil monster
2. Anti-hero/
antagonist
3. Trickster

Transformation
Archetypes:
1. Ritual bathing
2. Changing clothes
3. Death and rebirth
4. Rivers
5. Climbing mountains

Action Archetypes:
(Represent reaching for
metaphorical goals)
1. Tree
2. Bird

Figure 2–2c   Jungian Self Diagram (with answers)

construct a visual representation of the connection between the secondary archetypes and the primary archetypes of the self.

Again, my goal was to illustrate how these archetypes fit together. Of course, this was an objective classification and it could be argued that some of these images could fit together in different ways. For example, the trickster could take the place of the ego in some narratives. But once we filled in the blanks, students could better visualize this metaphorical code and develop the skills to crack it. Argument over the finer points of classification might come later as students began to practice archetypal criticism in earnest. The completed student version of the Jungian Self Diagram (Figure 2–2c) also became an important source of information throughout the unit as students learned to identify critical metaphors and see the underlying logic in interpreting them.

Connecting Archetypal Concepts

After students had worked through these activities, they were better prepared for the crux of the unit: understanding archetypes as a strategy for constructing meaning from text. We read anthologized versions of the Egyptian tale of Osiris and Isis, the Japanese folktale "Green Willow," the German folktale "The White Snake" (Albert et al. 1993, 35–51). I wanted to encourage students to talk about the archetypes, so students read all three tales within small groups. Each group was to informally discuss the secondary archetypes they identified and trace them back to the primary archetypes, thinking about what they might mean on a deeper level. I assigned a response paper asking students to organize and construct the ideas that stemmed from this discussion. While the written responses were somewhat tentative in tone, they showed evidence that students were experimenting with interpretive language and understood the basic concepts of archetypes. However, as the following writing excerpts illustrate, they stayed squarely within the safety of the story without delving into how those images and patterns elicited their response.

> The image of the tree and marriage are repeated throughout and provide vital insights into the characters' lives. The tree symbolizes the growth of the characters throughout the myth and the marriage is part of that growth. . . . The tree is a symbol of growth, fertility, creativity and regeneration. In each myth the tree symbolizes the love between the characters, it grows and the life of the tree follows the patterns of life for the characters. The marriage symbolizes the end of the search for each characters soulmate.
>
> —Sheri

As seen in "Osiris and Isis," "Green Willow," and "The White Snake," the ego, shadow and anima are all tied together to form a myth. Each archetype, or pattern, is brought out in a story. If one archetype were to be missing, the story would be left incomplete. The main character, the ego, creates a quest giving him/herself a goal to achieve. The shadow puts up obstacles creating challenges and barriers for the ego to break down. The anima balances the story by filling a void in the ego's life, giving him/her a reason to fight, a reason to fulfill their quest. They all need each other.

—Matt

The archetype of the forest is important because it is not only the drop-off point at which the heroes . . . begin their quest, but it also changes their lives and helps them to grow and achieve a personal paradise that all people subconsciously strive for.

—Sarah

Students had identified archetypes and made a connection to Jung's theories, even if their writing seemed somewhat detached, lacking the enthusiasm and authenticity of voice. Though their writing read like book reports, they were practicing archetypal theory, talking about the folktales in this theoretical language, and constructing meaning from the text.

Creation and Origin Mythology

Next, we moved to creation and origin mythology because it provided students the means to further examine archetypes quickly. These myths are short and the narrative patterns are more obvious than in longer texts. Creation mythology, of course, describes the genesis of the earth and the life forms that exist on it. Origin stories describe how things came to be; such as the introduction of evil into, and the subsequent destruction of, the newly created world. While details in such myths vary according to cultural and environmental factors, the basic archetypes of creation, origin, and destruction are remarkably similar. Joseph Campbell called these creation patterns the "cosmogonic cycle," arguing that these are the essential archetypes of origin mythology from all world cultures and represent "the passage of universal consciousness from the deep sleep . . . to the full day of waking; then back again . . . the life of the universe runs down and must be renewed" (1968, 266).

I used the concept of cosmogonic elements to help students interpret archetypes. Students read as many creation myths as they (or I) could stand (sources are noted at the end of this chapter), listing and responding to the similarities they found. After they had read several myths and discussed their lists in small groups, we brainstormed similarities as a class and categorized them into the big six: the (1) Beginning-less God who broods over the (2) Void and creates or discovers (3) Water and utters the (4) Sacred Sound, or Word, over the (5) Cosmic Egg to create life with a (6) Body Part.

Because students would be reading *Siddhartha* later in the unit, one of the myths I assigned was the Hindu Markandeya Purana creation myth. Later, this bit of knowledge helped to introduce the Indian ideology central to the novel. I include it here as a model for identifying cosmogonic elements, which are noted in brackets:

> In the beginning . . . Brahman existed independently of space-time [beginning-less god]. Akshara-Brahma, Brahma in the formless realm of pure ideas, first showed himself as a golden embryo of sound [sacred word]. He was a vowel, vibrating outward through nothingness [void]. The sound re-echoed back upon itself; its waves criss-crossed and became water [water element] and wind. The interplay of wind and water then began weaving the misty womb of the world [cosmic egg]. (Eliot 1976, 63)

It didn't take students long to say, "All right already! We get it. How many more of these do we have to read?" Reading the myths is the easy part, understanding them as metaphor for something difficult to comprehend, the origin of life and human consciousness, is something else.

I assigned Creating Creation: Writing Your Own Myth (Figure 2–3), requiring students to write their own creation myths and experiment with myth as metaphor. They would have ten minutes to tell their story of creation to the rest of the class, using visual aids to enhance their storytelling. I required them to include the six cosmogonic elements and an explanation of the culture they had created. I assessed them primarily on level of creativity and demonstrated knowledge of the archetypal elements of their myths.

When the time came to present their stories, students clearly exhibited that they had extended their knowledge of archetypal theory into their created worlds. This was memorably evident on the day when one group of three boys presented their myth to the class.

Taking center stage in the front of the classroom and casting sly glances at their captive audience, they prepared a large poster, a mixing bowl, and a pitcher of water as visuals for their presentation. The narrator began, "Before there was time, before there was motion, before there was food, there was the 'Big One.' He felt a strange sensation within him-

---

Creating Creation

Writing Your Own Myth

For this assignment, you'll write your own creation myth and present the story to the class. Model your creation on the myths we've read already, making sure you include all six of the cosmogonic elements we identified.

You will be graded on the following criteria:

- six elements included
- creativity of your myth
- an explanation of the culture you've created
- visual aids for storytelling
- written version to turn in

You will have ten minutes to present your myth in class. Your visual aid should enhance the telling of your tale.

Figure 2–3   Creating Creation: Writing Your Own Myth

© 2006 by Lisa Schade Eckert from *How Does It Mean?* Portsmouth, NH: Heinemann.

self as he gazed at the pure white nothingness around him, with only the sound of water in his ears." One boy swished the water around in the pitcher for effect. "He was moved to create new sterile white walls around the water which he called the Big Bowl." Another boy ceremoniously presented the empty bowl. "He saw that the Big Bowl was filled with water, and it was good." They paused dramatically after pouring the water into the bowl. Giggles broke out across the class as the metaphor for creation began to take shape: They had created their new world in a toilet bowl. This was definitely not the same version they had shared with me when we conferenced about their creation concept.

They watched me cringe as they described the sacred sound and told of the creation of the "cosmic egg" as it dropped into the bowl. "This is our start for archetypal criticism? Bathroom humor?!" I thought. "How will we make it through discussions of Joseph Campbell?" I wondered for a moment if perhaps I hadn't given them a bit too much wiggle room in the assignment. Should I stand up and be outraged? Should I lecture about what constitutes good taste? Was this best practice? But I was also having trouble keeping a straight face. I had to admire their creativity and their sense of fun and play with archetypes. After all, they had creatively met the requirements of the assignment and appropriated the concept of creation archetypes, making it their own. We had a good laugh while the next group prepared to present. This group had made a string of interconnected Crayola markers to illustrate the genesis of their society (der and wolley joined together create egnaro, and so on). It was hard to forget the cosmogonic elements after presentations like these.

After the last group had presented, I asked students to comment on what they had seen. They laughed about the funny ones and marveled at the different life forms that made it into our class. I assigned a group-response question: Did the myth create your culture or did your culture create the myth? They were stumped for a minute, but started thinking about how they actually came up with their stories. Some groups had to envision a culture before they could construct a myth they thought would be appropriate for that culture's genesis, while other groups quickly had their myth written and envisioned the culture that would spring from such a genesis. The discussion of their individual myth genesis turned to the origins of mythology. Did different societies or cultures create their myths in an attempt to impose order on the world, or did the ancient stories spawn societies in their individual images? This is the point at which students began to explore archetypes in myths as metaphors for universal events or beings that we cannot comprehend or explain.

We did get into some murky areas during the discussion of these questions, and it was here that we first began to critically discuss theory. I carefully defined the term *myth* at the beginning of this activity as "a story that gives people a code to live by" rather than a story that wasn't true. Because we were talking about issues of genesis, and we did read the book of Genesis as part of this unit, I was wary of offending religious sensibilities. An individual's sense of cultural and personal identity is tangled up in cultural mythology, and some students felt strongly about their religious background and had difficulty accepting the validity of the different cultural mythologies we read. But only one student openly voiced her religious objections, reducing the whole concept of archetypes to a discussion about creationism versus evolutionism. I pointed out that this was a theoretical approach to the text, not an argument for one theory of man's genesis over another. To argue that reading myths from an archetypal perspective is in some way blasphemous is to entirely miss the point of recognizing theory at all. Focusing on the archetype of creation itself has little to do with evolution. But the exchange raised a good point about using literary criticism as a central theme: I never emphasized a final reading, nor did I accept just any interpretation. In reality, any student who disagreed with an interpretation disagreed only with the approach, not necessarily with the work, me, or other members of the class. The archetypes of creation mythology certainly gave us ways of reading and the impetus for discussion. The student who objected came

---

Destruction Myth (Origin Myth)

After you have carefully created your society you must destroy it.

- include four origin archetypes (flood, the god's displeasure, paradise/hades, trickster)
- explain the introduction of evil
- explain how your culture is changed and enhanced by the experience
- present a brief (5-minute) presentation to tell your destruction story to the class

Response

Why are destruction myths also called origin myths? What does that say about the nature of destruction? Did your myth end on a negative or positive note?

Figure 2–4   Destruction Myth (Origin Myth)

© 2006 by Lisa Schade Eckert from *How Does It Mean?* Portsmouth, NH: Heinemann.

to the conclusion that the archetypal nature of creation stories proved that the Genesis account of creation must be true and, therefore, was the basis for all other mythology. Other students protested, but the argument centered on archetypal theory rather than religious dogma, enabling talk about these issues to center on a theoretical, not spiritual, basis.

After exploring the concept of creation, we moved on to the entrance of evil and destruction in mythology. Origin myths continue or complete the creation of the world and introduce the forces of evil and destruction. I patterned activities after the creation myth project; first, students read several origin myths, then listed recurring images and narrative patterns they had observed, then organized their observations into four categories: the great flood, the god's displeasure with earthly beings, the paradise/hades system of opposition (good versus evil), and the character of the trickster. Then they tackled the Destruction Myth project (Figure 2–4), in which they had to introduce evil into the world they created and tell the story of how the world was destroyed.

In the process, they had extended the metaphors from their creation myths. I assessed them on inclusion of the origin archetypes, the introduction of evil into the world, and a written explanation of how their culture was changed by the experience. I did not tell them they had to leave the door open for the reconstruction of a good and complete society; but interestingly, most of the stories they presented ended on a hopeful note. Destruction came in as many shapes and forms as creation. The boys with the "toilet world" flushed, and a new germ-free environment was created with the help of the Great One: Lysol. The Crayola group destroyed the world with a monster hurricane and flood, but ended with all the colors of the rainbow. It seemed to be almost instinctive for them that, as the new world is created, the possibility of a better life for the inhabitants exists. This laid the groundwork for discussing archetypes of transformation and renewal that would come later in the unit.

These myth projects opened for discussion the significance of archetypal patterns and what they mean to us, raising some profound questions. Did the student myths also communicate universal truths? What did their metaphors represent? How were they similar to the myths we read? The symbiotic relationship between destruction and creation provided fodder for discussion. Why must evil exist in every society's origin myth? How do we recognize goodness if there is no evil present in the world? Creation must occur for destruction to be possible, destruction must occur for the possibility of creating a better world. Students were engaged, most of them had completed assigned readings, they were actually talking about what they had read, and the transition into deeper theoretical ideas seemed less of a stretch.

The Heroic Journey

Our study of the heroic journey was modeled after that of Joseph Campbell, a noted comparative mythologist and Jungian scholar, and his analysis of the narrative structure of heroic epics in *The Hero with a Thousand Faces* (1968). His theories and diagrams provided a useful entry into an archetypal approach to the epic of Gilgamesh.

I introduced the concept of the heroic narrative structure by asking students to brainstorm a list of heroic characteristics, then note the archetypal patterns in most heroic tales and analyze their response to them. Then students traced these patterns back to the Jungian idea of self. Did the evil character fit the shadow archetypal pattern? Did the hero overcome difficult obstacles? Students recognized the hero genre readily, and had no trouble brainstorming different heroes from current movies and other stories they have read. They were quick to understand these characters and events as secondary archetypes, but the stretch to primary archetypes still required some guidance. I also recognized that students needed the opportunity to internalize aspects of the heroic by working through their own ideas, not just those that I had given them. We started with a small and familiar project: they created their own heroes. Using colored paper, markers, scissors, glue, magazines, and the other basic tools of the trade, we took a day in class to design a perfect hero. Students worked in small groups and each group gave their hero a name, then told a brief tale explaining their hero's exploits and heroic qualities.

The heroes developed predictably, often with cartoonish emphasis. There were the superheroes with muscles like rocks protruding absurdly from their bodies. One group's hero was an ordinary "nerd" with extraordinary (and secret) powers and a brain so large it needed to be supported by a special prosthetic. Another presented a hero that resembled a pro wrestler, complete with face paint and bravado. Women were represented as Amazonian, brilliant scientists, and supermoms.

"How can these heroes, all so different, each be a 'perfect' hero?" I asked students after we'd seen them all. "What do they have in common?"

Several students volunteer answers: "they're really strong or really smart"; "they're brave"; "they win fights" "they solve problems"; "they beat bad guys."

"Then why are they all so different?" I asked.

"Because we're all different" offered Tom.

"Some of your heroes have powers that humans don't have, like superheroes. What is the difference between a superhero and a hero?"

"A superhero isn't real. I know that I can't do any of the things a superhero can," Susan mused.

Jacob agreed. "Yeah, they don't really exist. There are heroes who are more like people who really lived."

"Which heroes were more inspiring to you?"

"The ones who are more like real people, who really did something. Like I wish I could be," Danielle decided.

"No way!" said Matt. "I want to be superman! I want to have lasers come out of my fingers and zap the school!"

Next, I showed *The Power of Myth: Episode I,* "The Hero's Adventure" with Joseph Campbell and TV reporter Bill Moyers (Campbell 1988). In the video, Campbell discusses all the major archetypes and uses them to interpret many different myths and folktales. The discussion provides several great examples of archetypal interpretation. The video appealed to students because it includes storytelling, clips from *Star Wars*, recent historical events, and lots of music. Students responded enthusiastically when Campbell encouraged all of us to follow our bliss.

We examined the heroic journey of our own lives before focusing on heroes far removed from our place and time. I asked them to think about the school year as a journey. What tasks or obstacles did they have to overcome? What rites of passage? How did they change or transform? I directed them to freewrite on either the journey of a year, a journey of a day, or even the entire four-year journey of high school.

Students volunteered all kinds of heroic acts they survived in high school. "Eating the lunches!" said Patrick. Others chimed in: "Getting through [football, soccer, track] season, " "passing algebra," "learning to drive," "going on your first date," "surviving a fight," "walking into the cafeteria all alone," "writing a research paper."

"Take out the lists of heroic characteristics you brainstormed earlier and find a partner. Compare those characteristics with the list of tasks your partner faces in the journey of a school year. What heroic characteristics does your partner demonstrate to get through a year or a day of school? For example, if Joe has to pass calculus successfully, that requires heroic stamina and brain power. Keep going from there."

They caught on quickly, and began comparing each other's lists. "You're a hero, man!" said Danielle to her partner. "You can do all these things!"

"How have these obstacles changed you?" I asked.

"I haven't changed at all," shrugged Tom. "I just get through it." His neighbor, Sara, retorted, "Then you need more obstacles!"

I asked them to identify their partner's heroic stature rather than their own at first for objectivity's sake. Many students had difficulty identifying themselves as heroes, while others wanted to exaggerate their heroic exploits. Once they compared their own and their partner's heroic traits required to make it through the journey of school, reluctant students could concede heroic stature and the more self-assured could justifiably proclaim it to the world. When they had compared notes, I asked them to respond to their heroics. Did they feel like heroes? How would they continue on their journeys? How were their own heroic traits similar to those of the hero they created? What "dragons" had they slain already? What dragons were looming in the near future? I hoped students would recognize aspects of themselves within the heroes they often admired and could use that self-knowledge when they read the heroic epic next. Maybe they would identify with the hero in a fundamental way, now that they saw themselves as somewhat heroic, too. Besides, this also emphasized the Jungian theory that the archetypes of heroes appeal to all of us; we love heroes because in reality we are all engaged in the heroic struggle of life. I diagrammed the heroic cycle loosely based on Joseph Campbell's diagram of the adventure (1968, 245) (Figure 2–5), and we talked about the heroes they had listed earlier. Would they designate various heroes as spiritual, reluctant, or physical? Could they trace this heroic journey to see if they fit with the heroic cycle depicted in the diagram?

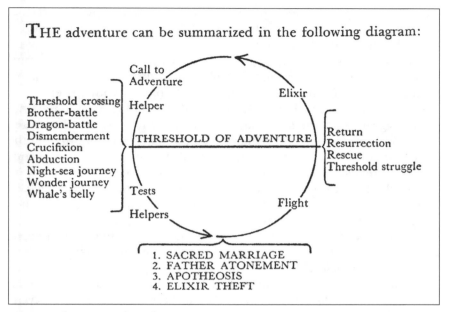

THE adventure can be summarized in the following diagram:

Call to
Adventure

Elixir

Threshold crossing   Helper
Brother-battle
Dragon-battle
Dismemberment   THRESHOLD OF ADVENTURE
Crucifixion   Return
Abduction   Resurrection
Night-sea journey   Rescue
Wonder journey   Threshold struggle
Whale's belly   Tests

Helpers   Flight

1. SACRED MARRIAGE
2. FATHER ATONEMENT
3. APOTHEOSIS
4. ELIXIR THEFT

Figure 2–5   Heroic Cycle Diagram

Gilgamesh: Mapping the Journey

Studying *Gilgamesh* encouraged students to look more closely at specific archetypes in the hero motif. It is important to note it is not essential that *Gilgamesh* be used here as the epic text; actually any of the heroic epics will work. Methods outlined here are appropriate and easily adaptable to various world epics outlined in any curriculum. This way, students can identify secondary archetypes on their own, and classroom discussion and activities emphasize connections to primary archetypes. *Gilgamesh* is a rich tale, full of adventure and imagery, and it worked well as a means of assessing student progress.

   Gilgamesh is an heroic epic from ancient Mesopotamia and involves a cast of gods, goddesses, men, monsters, and animals. Found in most world literature anthologies, extensive myth and legend anthologies, and hero anthologies, the epic has been widely translated in forms varying from simplified prose narratives to highly complex analyses of poetry and variants. I used a combination of the excerpts in the Holt, Rinehart and Winston *World Literature* (1993) text and supplemental passages from both David Ferry's (1992) and John Gardner's (Gardner and Maier 1984) translations. The textbook's prose translation is easy to read, Ferry's is accessible poetry, and Gardner's is very detailed with many critical sources that a teacher might find useful.

We started with the study guide Heroic Quest Archetypes: Diagramming the Hero's Journey (Figure 2–6) to help them clarify ideas as we read *Gilgamesh*. The guide is versatile enough to work with any epic text, and we also used it for Herman Hesse's *Siddhartha* (1982) later in the unit. Following the guide helped students focus their reading, and I required them to keep a log of archetypal events they considered important to the development of character and narrative structure. Using these events, students created a diagram of the heroic quest, modeled somewhat on Campbell's heroic cycle (Figure 2–5). I encouraged them to visualize Gilgamesh's heroic path, designing its structural representation as they imagined it should look. Creating a diagram for Gilgamesh's heroic cycle was a creative way for students to understand the patterns of the epic, and was useful for comparisons later with George Lucas' Star Wars films as well as with *Siddhartha*. We worked in small groups, sharing various diagrams in class, but this could easily be accomplished as an individual project. Most groups began with circular diagrams (it is the heroic cycle, after all!), but soon began to branch out into angles and arcs as Gilgamesh continued on his quest.

The first step in understanding an epic archetypically is to establish the cast of characters. The secondary archetypes of the hero, the sidekick, the helpful god or goddess, the villains or monsters, and the love interest are all symbolic of the primary archetypes of the unconscious mind. In this case, obviously, Gilgamesh, the two-parts-man and one-part-god king of Uruk, is the hero. He was created by the gods to be perfect: he is beautiful, strong, brave, and intelligent, but unfortunately, a very arrogant and crass ruler. Because of his arrogance, his people ask the gods to humble him by sending a stronger man to challenge his authority. The gods comply by creating Enkidu, a wild man from the woods, out of their saliva and some dirt and pine needles. Enkidu comes out of the woods to challenge Gilgamesh to a wrestling match, which Gilgamesh wins. The god Shamash is Gilgamesh's guiding force, and helps him in times of trouble. Students who have had some experience with archetypes already begin to notice evident patterns. Enkidu, wild, dirty, and aggressive, and therefore an easily recognizable shadow, comes from the forest, an archetype symbolizing the unconscious mind. Because Gilgamesh wins the wrestling match, he has essentially overpowered his shadow and assimilated him into the conscious area of his self, his first step toward individuation or self-knowledge. After he is beaten in the wrestling match, Enkidu complements Gilgamesh's persona. Consequently, Gilgamesh becomes a fairer and more just ruler because Enkidu becomes his loyal

Heroic Quest Archetypes
Diagram the Hero's Journey

Mythologists have noted that most heroic quests contain some very similar archetypal plot characteristics and events, many of which are outlined in Joseph Campbell's books and comments. Archetypal Criticism invites comparison of heroic quest to find the deeper significance of the hero to the reader.

Part I: Archetype Log

Your assignment now is to keep a log of archetypal events in which the hero is involved as you are reading/viewing the hero tale. The following archetypal events should be noted as you critically follow the quest:

- The call to adventure: is this a reluctant, physical or spiritual hero? What event(s) starts the adventure?
- Threshold of adventure: when does the hero "jump off" into the unknown? Where is the point of no return?
- Descent into the abyss: when does hero find himself at his lowest point? Is it a physical or spiritual abyss?
- Slaying monsters/dragons: how many obstacles lie in the hero's path? How does he meet these obstacles?
- Transformations: how many times does the hero undergo a change? Are they physical or spiritual changes?
- Look for change of clothes, ritual bathing, crossing of rivers or mountains, etc. . . .
- The return: does the hero return to the point from which he started? How is he different at the end?

Character types are also important to the archetypal pattern of a story. In addition to plot design, record different characters and the primary archetypes they represent as you experience the story. You should note the following archetypes:

- ego: usually the main character, the hero
- shadow: the adversary of the hero
- anima/us: the character of the opposite sex that is somehow involved with the hero

Part II: Diagram the Quest

Once you have noted the archetypal events and characters listed above, you are ready to begin to construct your diagram of this specific heroic quest and its archetypal

continued

Figure 2–6   Heroic Quest Archetypes: Diagram the Hero's Journey

significance. Your diagram may be in any shape or form, but it must be logical for your hero's journey. Be sure you include the archetypes you have noted and clearly label them. You may construct this diagram as a model, poster, drawing, etc. . . . But the end result should reflect careful thought, creativity, and neatness.

Response

How does this hero tale compare to others you have read/viewed? Could you use the model you've created to illustrate a different story, or would you have to make major changes in design? What conclusions can you draw about the heroic tale?

What is the ultimate significance of the heroic quest to the reader? What lesson are we to learn from the hero's experiences?

Figure 2–6 *continued*

and trusted sidekick and helps him to see both sides of any issue. This is Gilgamesh's first transformation, or his first step on the road to individuation or self-knowledge.

Because Gilgamesh recognizes Enkidu as his shadow or alter-ego, he is devastated when Enkidu dies. In essence, a part of his consciousness has been taken from him. The death of Enkidu provides Gilgamesh with his quest for immortality because he is afraid to die; Enkidu glimpsed the underworld in a dream and found it to be a desolate place. Students should recognize several archetypal patterns in this section of the epic. First, Enkidu's dream is the archetypal descent into the underworld or the descent deep into the subconscious to confront one of mankind's deepest fears: the unknown transformation of death, a pattern all heroes in mythology undergo. Second, just as his fear of the unknown was exemplified in the Cedar Forest, Gilgamesh still greatly fears the unknown in the world of death, an indication to the reader that he is not fully self-actualized and still has much to overcome.

The final section of the epic completes the heroic cycle as Gilgamesh finds Utnapishtim, the only human who has been granted immortality. Gilgamesh returns to Uruk as a wiser man to write down his story. Students recognized the archetypes of the flood, river, the flower, ritual bathing and changing of clothes, and Gilgamesh's deep descent into unconsciousness as he dives into the river to retrieve the magic plant. It is not insignificant that a serpent steals the plant; snakes are archetypal tricksters, and it is the snake who sheds his skin in continual transformation to become "new" again.

When Gilgamesh returns to Uruk, he is also a changed man. He is no longer a crass young ruler, but a wise and gracious king who spends his last years writing his story to enlighten future generations. This is the archetypal return; the hero comes back as a self-actualized and mature individual to the place where he began. This raises the question: Did Gilgamesh complete his quest? Taken literally, no he didn't. He did not bring back the secret of immortality. But he did overcome his fears, mature into a wise and fair ruler, and understand who and what he really is. Some students argued that he did find the ultimate secret to immortality: he wrote down his story and we were still talking about and learning from him, therefore he was immortal. It made for an interesting class discussion and indicated that students were understanding the heroic cycle as a metaphor for our own journey through life. Just as the creation myths presented the "unknowable" through metaphor, so does the heroic epic. Why must we be born only to grow old and die? What are we put on this earth to accomplish? Why does the human race seem to make many of the same mistakes over and over again? We pulled out the personal hero responses again. How is the journey through the school year similar to Gilgamesh's journey? How is each student the same or different at the end of the year? What does this mean about the importance of the journey?

As we read the epic, the logic of archetypal interpretation truly dawned on students. I loved the time we spent on Gilgamesh because students truly began to apply archetypal images and events to their own lives. Take the day Ashley bounced into class with the movie *Hook*, starring Robin Williams, as an example:

"I watched this with the kids I baby-sat last night. I can't believe how many archetypes are in this movie!" she gushed, breathlessly. "At the beginning, Peter doesn't even know who he is, and he doesn't really believe what everyone says until he gets hit in the head with a baseball. Then he descends into the cave under the tree, looks into the water and bam! suddenly knows who he is! That's just like the other heroes. He has to look into his unconscious mind and he can't do it all by himself. This is so cool! I was jumping up and down, the kids thought I was nuts!"

Ashley's friend Melanie attested to her enthusiasm. "Yeah, she called me then. She kept saying, 'Archetypes, archetypes!' It was so funny!"

"Can we watch the part?" Ashley begged. "I know right where it is. It will only take a few minutes. Please?" The class clamored for the movie. So we watched, and she was right. The heroic descent into the abyss was perfectly illustrated. I just sat quietly as the class discussed

Peter's epiphany and sudden actualization. "He's changed forever," said Dan. "I've seen this before; he throws away his cell phone and turns into a great dad." I was reminded of Danielle, the student who came to class one day after watching *The Fugitive* with Harrison Ford. "I see these things everywhere!" she had sighed. "You've ruined movies for me!" I was a little overwhelmed; they were cognitively theorizing by generalizing the tenets of archetypal theory into other texts and areas of their lives. I did feel a little remorse at the "ruining movies" part, but took that as a sign of her more mature, critical view of the world. When we moved on to different schools of literary theory they would already have a knowledge base from which to start. This was evident in another brief classroom exchange:

"You know, lots of the stories I read when I was kid had these things in them," mused Angie. "Think of *Alice in Wonderland*, or *The Wizard of Oz*. Alice and Dorothy go through the same things."

"Why do you think we like these stories so much?" I asked.

"Because we all go through the same thing! We are always trying to figure out who we are and what we want. And all of the people in these stories get to figure it out by the end."

We were really getting somewhere.

Star Wars as Best Practice?

Another epic tale that clearly illustrates epic and archetypal pattern is, of course, the Star Wars trilogy. Watching the Star Wars movies turned out to be a great way to capitalize on student interest in archetypes. The first movie, *Star Wars*, is the most basic representation of the heroic quest, but in *Return of the Jedi*, Luke actually achieves individuation. I didn't expect the response I received when we first talked about watching excerpts of the movie. I had planned to use one class period to show significant clips, but the class had other ideas. First they just wanted to watch the entire *Star Wars* movie, but then . . .

"Can we watch more than just the first movie? Please?"

"What?!" I laughed, not thinking they were serious. "We don't have time to watch *two* movies in a row! Plus we'd get bored. Rent them and watch them at home."

"We want to watch it together, here. How can we talk about the hero cycle when we don't see the end of it? We need to at least see *Return of the Jedi*."

"How could we ever find the time to do that? You'd have to do your work on your own time. We only have three days next week, and you'd use them all up with another movie."

They considered this, and a small debate erupted. I listened, incredulous. But overwhelmingly, the class wanted to watch the extra movie. I couldn't believe they were serious. Was this just a ploy to use up class time? I didn't allow students to work on homework or other assignments in my class unless the time is reserved for that. I also didn't show many movies, opting to show relevant excerpts instead. I glanced at the kids who usually want to get right to work and avoid homework as much as possible. They were just as enthusiastic.

"Why?" I asked. "You've already seen these movies a hundred times, and the special effects aren't even all that great anymore."

"We love those movies!"

"Why?" I asked again. I was intrigued. Maybe there was a lesson in the appeal of the heroic to our subconscious here.

"Because they're awesome! I love all of the creatures and planets," said Matt. "I like the light sabers!" said Jeremy. They sensed my interest, pressed for an advantage.

"I don't know why, I would just like to watch them here, so we can talk about stuff," said Angie.

"After Joseph Campbell talked about them in the video, I really want to watch them again. I want to see if it really has all those archetypes," said Matt.

"I'll have to think about it," I said, lamely, trying to deflect and move on to something else.

"We'll work hard for the rest of the year!" someone promised. Sure you will, I thought cynically; but I was impressed by their vehemence and their unity. Why did these movies have such appeal?

Suddenly I found myself wanting to watch the movies with them, to continue sharing the experience of the heroic archetypes. "Well, you'll have to diagram the journey," I warned, to justify the use of time, certain that the reality of the extra work would deter them. It didn't work.

"We will!" they whooped, almost in unison.

As we settled in to watch the movies, I sighed to myself, feeling guilty, and wondered if this could in any way be considered best practice. How many parents would call, wondering why we just watched movies all the time in English class? I knew I'd hear about it in the teacher's lunch room. But watching both movies was great. We truly became a community of learners experiencing the movies together, discussing the archetypes of the hero tale as something "craved" by the collective unconscious, and our instinctive response to them. They even asked to stop the movie at times to point out archetypal events (when I did that with movie excerpts, they usually found it annoying). They understood the movie in an entirely new way, though students could rent and watch these movies at any time and many had seen them over and over again.

Applying Archetypal Theory

What if they had to figure out how to use archetypal theory as a framework on their own, without my specific direction? I gave them Gabriela Mistral's short story "Why Reeds Are Hollow" as a quiz, directing them to write a brief archetypal analysis. The story is very short, so one class period allows enough time for reading and interpretation; we returned to this story several times throughout the year to apply and compare different theoretical approaches and the resulting interpretations. It contains both obvious and subtle archetypes so students of various levels can feel challenged and successful. The object was for students to locate, examine, and interpret archetypal characters or events in the story during one class period. The prompt for the piece didn't need to be long or elaborate; students were simply instructed to interpret the story/poem from an archetypal perspective. Because students were becoming more aware of their interpretive processes, responses became more authentic as students became more engaged with their reading and wrote what they really thought. I knew we were accomplishing something when I received responses like Kristi's:

> From an archetypal approach, this is a story of death and rebirth. In the beginning, everything is alive, but soon things die because the reeds are greedy and want to be equally as tall as the trees. After six months, however, the land is reborn . . . the new order is established by "the River God [who] appeared after a long absence and, rejoicing, sang of a new era." The river is an archetype because it represents the transitional phases of life and the flowing of time into eternity. There was a transitional phase of life when things died and came back. Nature is supposed to be forever like the irreversible passage of time.

Owning *Siddhartha*

Students were progressing in their understanding of archetypes, and that the same patterns are found in all genres of storytelling, not just mythology. We wrapped up the unit by applying archetypal interpretation to a novel. An archetypal/Jungian critic would argue, of course, that any novel is appropriate, but I used *Siddhartha*, by Hermann Hesse (1982), for many reasons, not the least of which was because there was an old classroom set in the English storage room, and I knew none of the students had read it in class before. I also chose this novel because it built on the mythic foundation that had been established throughout the unit and engaged student interest for a quick read. *Siddhartha* is the story of Siddhartha Gothama, also known as Buddha. It is an heroic adventure much like Luke Skywalker's and Gilgamesh's adventures, but Siddhartha is a spiritual hero on a quest of the soul. Just as with the other heroes we studied, the psychological development of Siddhartha mirrors the psychological development of the individual. Students quickly recognized Siddhartha as a spiritual hero and drew on their experiences with *Gilgamesh* and the *Star Wars* movies to identify his heroic transformations throughout his quest.

It became immediately apparent that students were engaging with this novel with an enthusiasm that surprised even them. The story touched on the concept of self, and they were at point in their lives when they were trying to determine just who they were anyway. Shortly after we began reading the novel, Danielle asked if she could buy her book. "I want to make notes in it. And I want to keep it."

"That's a great idea," said Matt. "We just won't turn them in at the end of the year."

"How many of you would like to buy a copy?" I asked. Almost every hand went up. "Are you serious? Why do you want to keep it?"

"I don't know," said Tom, "I just want to." The class murmured in agreement.

I stopped by the office after class to ask the secretary if they could just buy the books. She blanched, saying that it would be far too much paperwork at the end of the year to have to collect money for and reorder an entire classroom set of books. I relayed the message to the class the next day.

"Then let's order them," Danielle decided. "We can just do it ourselves. We'll buy new ones and keep these. How many people can bring in money? We can just order them from a bookstore." She organized a list and checked off names of students who wanted to buy the book. Sure enough, most of the students had brought in money by the end of the week. I worried about the few students who couldn't afford to bring in money to buy one, but solved the problem by just letting them keep the school copy, figuring that I could note them as lost at the end of the year.

I called a local bookstore and ordered the copies, but students didn't want to wait for a new copy and were satisfied with keeping the older ones as their own. When the new ones finally arrived, I just put them on my shelf. Students kept the copies of the novel they had been reading and making notes in, and the main office was never the wiser. Many of these students hadn't read an entire book in a very long time, not to mention buying one with their own money. These were inexpensive paperbacks, but the idea that they wanted the book that badly made quite an impression on me. Here was tangible evidence that students were taking responsibility for their learning. And the story of Siddhartha's journey made an impression on them, which became apparent in their informal written responses.

Matt wrote, "Siddhartha was the ego. He was on a quest 'to become empty of thirst, desire, dreams, pleasure, and sorrow—to let the Self die'(14). The whole story revolved around him and 'the troubled course of the life cycle' (15)." In other words, his quest is one of individuation. Sarah decided that "[the] anima in the story of Siddhartha was Kamala. . . . she depended on him for caring and guidance in her life. He helped her become happy and knowledgeable." Indeed, Kamala seemed the picture of an anima, sitting temptingly in her garden and transforming Siddhartha with one kiss. But students puzzled over the shadow. Some pointed to Siddhartha's father or Vasudeva, the river man. Angie, who referred to the shadow as "the insanity of one's being," identified the inner nature of Siddhartha's self as the shadow in the novel.

His own evil was his mind. It was what he was constantly struggling with. He 'was afraid of [himself. He] was fleeing from [himself]. [He] was seeking Brahman, Atman, . . . [he] wished to get away from [himself] in order to find in the unknown innermost, the nucleus of all things . . . his own self being' (38). He was battling the feelings and thoughts that gathered within himself. When he overcame his inner self he was able to let his outer self live.

This touched off a vehement debate on the subject. While some students pointed to Siddhartha's father as the shadow and others identified Vasudeva, there was a small Govinda contingent, arguing that Govinda was Siddhartha's opposite or, as one student put it, "Siddhartha's mirror reflection" and, therefore, his shadow. When Siddhartha decides not to follow Gotama, Govinda does the opposite and stays with the Enlightened One; when Siddhartha is at his lowest ebb and contemplating suicide, he awakens to find Govinda calmly sitting by his side; when Siddhartha finds his salvation in the end of the novel, Govinda is still seeking and trying to understand. Siddhartha becomes free of the worldly desires and one with the universe while Govinda is helplessly overcome. Here was a critical argument, in which students rationally presented and listened to each other's views; we never came to a full agreement, but the argument was satisfying.

Some students returned to the Heroic Quest guide to record patterns and images as they identified them. Using the same worksheet with *Siddhartha* as they did with *Gilgamesh* enabled them to comfortably find similarities and differences in the heroic quests and symbolism in each of the works. Some students wanted to create "submodels" of the journey. Instead of one large diagram, they might model only Siddhartha's father quest, assimilation of anima, assimilation of ego, experience with collective unconscious, or one of his many transformations. Others didn't use any of the guides at all; they just read and responded to the novel within the framework of archetypal theory.

Approaching *Siddhartha* archetypically established a reading purpose, helping students see the "point" of an otherwise mystifying novel. Students also recognized elements of their own lives in Siddhartha's struggle to understand himself and the world around him. Siddhartha finds enlightenment as he understands the difference between knowledge (or wisdom) and learning. Knowledge is found within an individual and can be brought to the surface (to "educe" as in "educate" means to "bring out") but learning is the process of making sense of the knowledge others offer to help individuals recognize their own wisdom. Siddhartha chooses the path of knowledge and experiences the difficulty of traveling his path without learning the way from a guide or teacher. In the end he recognizes the importance of learning from others. Katie, a student who had always experienced great difficulty in English classes before, was particularly struck by Siddhartha's reflections on learning from his father. She wrote:

> Siddhartha starts out by leaving his father to find out who he really is, why he is here. This is what starts the father quest or cycle of life. '. . . something in this reflection that reminded him of something he had forgotten and when he reflected on it, he remembered . . . His face . . . resembled the face of his father, the Brahmin' (131). Siddhartha is now realizing he has fulfilled the quest of the cycle of life. He now has a son that [sic] did the exact same thing he did to his dad when he was younger. He has reached that point and taken over a new role.

It seemed that by the time we finished *Siddhartha*, students had developed a sensitivity to archetypes that enabled them to use the method with any text. I was somewhat bound to the works included in this chapter by the World Literature curriculum. But opportunities for stretching the canon using an archetypal approach are limited only by time, money, and curricular expectations.

Focusing specifically on archetypal theory helped students understand why they respond to literature, why literature touches the deepest reaches of the reader's unconscious mind, and why the reader identifies so closely with the hero of a story. It became easier for them to make connection to texts outside the realm of literature, and they were suddenly standing back and "reading" the world critically as they noticed and constructed meaning from recurrent patterns of imagery. Most important, though, they actually read. They didn't know why they found reading *Siddhartha* so captivating, but having a purpose for reading certainly helped. Learning about archetypes also proved useful as a basis for introducing the larger concept of literary theory. As Frye says, "An archetype should not be only a unifying category of criticism, but itself a part of the total form, and it leads us at once to the question of what sort of total form criticism can see in literature" (2001, 1450).

I learned a great deal from this unit about theory, teaching, and also myself. I had left behind the anthology and the study guides and had let student inquiry guide the interpretation of *Siddhartha*. Students could "wield the theory" not only as a reading strategy coming from an outside source (me), but also as a means for identifying and articulating their own response to the text. And I found myself looking forward to my World Literature class every day.

Further Teaching Suggestions

- Video games often depict archetypal characters and quests. Ask students to consider the ways in which archetypes are represented in video-game narratives.

- Using anthologies of world mythology and folktales, have students read and locate a myth, legend, or folktale from another country. Then they can prepare a class presentation in which they tell the story, locate archetypal characters and patterns, and share the ways in which these archetypes help them to understand the story. This helps the class gain practice in identifying and analyzing archetypes, make connections between myth narratives from around the world, and hear a number of good stories.

- Model an archetypal reading of comic or anime books, or allow students to work with this genre.

More Readings for Teaching Archetypal Theory

The Deadliest Game by Tom Clancy (YA Net Force series)

His Dark Materials trilogy by Phillip Pullman (*The Golden Compass*, in particular)

Jane Eyre by Charlotte Brontë

Redwall by Brian Jacques

The True Confessions of Charlotte Doyle by Avi

Wuthering Heights by Emily Brontë

And certainly the Harry Potter books!

Mythology Sources

Abrahams, Roger D. 1983. *African Folktales: Traditional Stories of the Black World*. New York: Pantheon Books.

Amor, Anne Clark. 1975. *Beasts and Bawdy*. New York: Taplinger.

Asimov, Isaac. 1961. *Words from the Myths*. Boston: Houghton Mifflin.

Astrow, Margot. 1972. *American Indian Prose and Poetry*. New York: John Day.

Bettelheim, Bruno. 1976. *The Uses of Enchantment*. New York: Alfred A. Knopf.

Botkin, Benjamin A. 1944. *A Treasury of American Folklore*. New York: Crown.

Campbell, Joseph. 1986. *The Inner Reaches of Outer Space: Metaphor as Myth and as Religion*. New York: A. Van der March Editions.

Campbell, Joseph. 1970. *Myths, Dreams, and Religion*. New York: E. P. Dutton.

Cavendish, Richard, ed. 1982. *Legends of the World*. First American Edition. New York: Schocken.

Cavendish, Richard, ed. 1992. *Mythology: An Illustrated Encyclopedia*. New York: Little, Brown.

Chevalier, Jean. 1994. *A Dictionary of Symbols*. Oxford, MA: Blackwell.

Dorson, Richard Mercer. 1961. *Folk Legends of Japan*. Rutland, VT: C. E. Tuttle.

Eberhard, Wolfram. 1965. *Folktales of China*. Chicago: University of Chicago Press.

Eliot, Alexander. 1976. *The Universal Myths: Heroes, Gods, Tricksters and Others*. New York: Meridian.

Erdoes, Richard and Alfonso Ortiz, eds. 1984. *American Indian Myths and Legends*. New York: Pantheon Books.

Hamilton, Virginia. 1988. *In the Beginning: Creation Stories from Around the World*. New York: Harcourt Brace Jovanovich.

Rolleston, T. W. *Celtic Myths and Legends*. 1990. New York: Dover.

Schoolcraft, Henry Rowe. 1969. *The Fire Plume*. New York: The Dial Press.

Stillman, Peter R. 1985. *Introduction to Myth*. 2d ed. Portsmouth, NH: Boynton/Cook.

van Buitenen, J. A. B. 1959. *Tales of Ancient India*. Chicago: University of Chicago Press.

3 Structure and Sense: Teaching Students Objective Theory

Texts are made of words, not things or ideas.
—Michael Riffaterre

The skeptics among my students love objectivity. It's appealing to seek the "one real meaning" of a story or poem, and comforting for students who look for "a bottom line." These were students who had been confounded by the emotional and psychological aspects of determining literary meaning and merit, who suspiciously asked questions like, "How can this mean different things to different people?" or "What is the *real* meaning? How can you prove it?" They welcomed an approach advocating scientific and objective evaluation. Before I began to teach with literary theory, I always felt like I was vacillating between two extremes when I taught literature: I would either encourage students to focus on how a work would make them "feel," sometimes causing them to rejoice, like Tom in the first chapter, that the nebulous world of metaphor and connotation meant they could "BS" their way through English class (I have more to say on this in the next chapter); or I would emphasize a close reading, spoon-feeding an examination of metaphor and symbolism to ensure that students stood in awe of both the literature itself and my command of interpreting it. I was never really satisfied with either of these approaches in isolation. Of course, I encourage student response and love when a student becomes personally engaged in a work of literature. But there is also much to be valued in learning that texts don't just "happen," they are crafted; recognizing the structural elements that construct a text and, consequently, provide meaning should be a part of every student's repertoire of interpretive strategies. I wanted to teach objective theory, not merely enforce or defend close reading for the "right" meaning. Teaching such text-based strategies in relation to other interpretive methods as part of an overall repertoire of meaning-making strategies can actually help students identify why they respond to text at all.

Essentials of Objective Theory

Objectivism is a term that incorporates theories of reading and literary interpretation that emphasize textual form over subjective experience.

M. H. Abrams defines objective criticism as an approach that recognizes a text "as something which stands free from reference to the poet, the audience, and the environing world. It describes the literary product as a self-sufficient and autonomous object, or else as a world-in-itself . . ." (1988, 40). In this case, a hero can only be judged by his actions in a specific plot, not by comparison to the many heroes who came before him. A "tree" is a large plant, not an archetypal symbol of life and certainly not an invitation for nostalgic reminiscences of childhood on the part of the reader. The text is the thing; no personal experience, societal background, or author intentions are relevant. A word means what it means, regardless of what the author might have intended or the reader associates with the word. "The poem . . . is not your experience or my experience; it is only a potential cause of experiences, and the adequacy of any subjective response must be tested against the 'objective' poem itself" (Kermode 1987, 77). Instead of focusing on what is happening in the mind as meaning is constructed, the reader focuses attention on the text, examining how language creates meaning. To probe and test through the specifics of language, to challenge ourselves to new intellectual and artistic levels, lifts us to the level of the work instead of bringing the work to our level.

Essentially, an objective approach boils down to understanding the two levels of linguistic meaning that are part of everyday communication: deep structure and surface structure. A novel, short story, or poem must follow certain basic conventions both in the deeper structure of genre and the surface structures of words and phrases. An objective reader "refuses the 'obvious' meaning of the story and seeks instead to isolate 'deep' structures within it, which are not apparent on the surface" (Eagleton 1996, 83). Introduction of setting, character, conflict, and basic situation, followed by plot sequences leading to a resolution of conflict, provide the underlying structure of a short story or novel. The surface structure of irony, metaphor, symbolism, and grammar creates and reinforces suspense and tension. Objective approaches to literary interpretation include structuralist, formalist, and New Critical theories. I did not differentiate specifically between these approaches in my classroom, nor will I here, but I incorporated concepts from each to present the basic arguments for text-based construction of meaning as opposed to the more affective methods, like archetypal or response theory.

Teaching Objective Theory

Reviewing students' prior knowledge of literary conventions served as a starting point for introducing this unit, which took about four weeks. When I asked students, as a preliminary exercise, to help me outline the basic structure of a story on an overhead transparency, they remembered the plot structure they'd been learning for years (with a little prompting). I drew the traditional bell curve and we labeled the appropriate parts as exposition or basic situation, complications or rising action, climax, falling action, and resolution or denouement.

"What happens if an element of the plot structure is missing, or if the author switched them all around?" I asked. "You'd have to try and figure it out," said one student. "But you might just decide it was stupid, and stop reading."

"What if the reader never really could figure out the basic situation, or there was no resolution in a story?" I pressed. "Same thing," offered another. "You'd think the book was stupid. I'd be mad that I wasted my time!"

"So, why is the basic structure of a work so important?"

"It's the same thing as a movie, or TV. You want to see what happens to the people. I hate those kind of movies where nothing really happens. And when I have to read something that just goes on and on, I get bored."

Then, taking out blank transparencies, I said, "OK, let's think back to *Siddhartha*. What specific words from the novel come to your mind?" As they volunteered names, places, and events, I wrote them in red on the overhead, purposefully putting them in a chronologically ordered curve, parallel to the plot structure curve I'd drawn earlier. I stepped back, and we looked at the words that seemed littered on the page. "If you didn't know that story, what would you think of these words here?" They stared at me, blankly. Then I put the blue plot structure transparency on top of it, and said, "Does this structure help you make sense of the red *Siddhartha* words?" They recognized that the blue plot structure enabled the seemingly random words in red to make sense.

"It's like a skeleton!" said Kristi, referring to the basic plot structure. Both the bell curve and the random words are brought to life in the way the basic skeletal structure of the human body is brought to life by a circulatory, nervous, and gastrointestinal system. These systems rely on one another to form the larger structure of the body; even a small blood or brain cell contributes specifically to a body's systems, just like specific words in a literary work contribute to the story or poem as a whole. I handed out an Objective Theory guide (Figure 3–1), and we continued the discussion. "It's like an ecosystem. If you add or take something away, it can screw up the whole food chain. We just learned about that in earth science," said Ryan. "That's why zebra mussels are big trouble for the Great Lakes." Students thought of other analogies comparing architecture, chemistry, and mathematics to objective literary theory. When we really began to parse terms like "systems" and "structure," I

Objective Theory

Objective criticism is a method that utilizes specific language systems from the text to judge literary merit. This method intends to make the study of literature more scientific and uniform. As opposed to an archetypal approach in which the reader looks for common patterns in all literature, approaching a text objectively means focusing attention on the language from only a single work of literature.

In this view, attention is focused on the way the text is constructed. "Structures" in literature are just like concrete structures in the world around you: they are built of different pieces and materials. The materials used to build structures in literature are words, sentences, chapters, stanzas, themes, symbols, and different elements of the plot. Interpretation is limited to only what the structure relates and not to any reality existing outside of the text itself. The reader accepts meanings *denoted* by words and phrases instead of relying on individual *connotations* based on personal experience or associations in constructing meaning.

A Model of Structural Analysis

There are two basic layers of literary meaning. The bottom layer is the essential, but often invisible, defining structure of a work. The top layer is the essential and often studied language that enables the structure of literary convention to work. For a work to be satisfying, thrilling, suspenseful, funny, or cathartic, the layers of meaning must compliment one another. The basic structure directs and supports the words of the text, while the words embellish the basic structure. When the layers are well constructed, we enjoy the work and hardly even notice their existence as we skim along and lose ourselves in the story world!

Surface Layers of Meaning (there can be many of these)—The language of a text (metaphor, irony, description, imagery, rhyme, and so on) which embellishes the underlying structure.

Deep Layer of Meaning (there can be only one of these)—The underlying structural layer which defines work as poem (with stanzas), short story or novel (with a basic plot structure), or drama (with acts and scenes) and enables the surface layer of meaning to exist.

Remember, the text is the thing. Denotations (also known as dictionary definitions) of words are important, therefore the dictionary should not be far from your side as you read. You must determine which meaning denoted by the dictionary is most appropriate within the context of both linguistic structures. To be objective means the connotations you personally associate with a word are not necessarily appropriate!

Figure 3–1   Objective Theory

knew students were ready to try their hand at objective interpretation as a reading strategy, not just as directed analysis or right-or-wrong answers to literal questions.

"Fifteen"

I liked the poem "Fifteen," by William Stafford, because students could recognize the obvious systems of repetition and metaphor to reach some conclusions about the meaning of the text and it was short enough to cover in one class period. My purpose was to model an objective reading for students before turning them loose to practice it on their own. I wanted to help students understand how to use linguistic systems to determine the meaning of a work so they could understand objective theory as another way of comprehending text, to show students the difference in connotation and denotation, and illustrate the ways in which we must consider both levels of language to accurately interpret specific words.

Fifteen

WILLIAM STAFFORD

South of the bridge on Seventeenth
I found back of the willows one summer
day a motorcycle with engine running
as it lay on its side, ticking over
slowly in the high grass. I was fifteen.

I admired all that pulsing gleam, the
shiny flanks, the demure headlights
fringed where it lay; I led it gently
to the road and stood with that
companion, ready and friendly. I was fifteen.

We could find the end of a road, meet
the sky on out Seventeenth. I thought about
hills, and patting the handle got back a
confident opinion. On the bridge we indulged
a forward feeling, a tremble. I was fifteen.

Thinking, back farther in the grass I found
the owner, just coming to, where he had flipped
over the rail. He had blood on his hand, was pale—
I helped him walk to his machine. He ran his hand
over it, called me a good man, roared away.

I stood there, fifteen.

Application

1. First, look for overall structural patterns and stanza configuration.

2. Then look closely at each stanza. What linguistic structures do you notice in each? Look for metaphor, descriptive words, word placement, meter and rhyme, and imagery.

3. Why is the phrase "I was fifteen" repeated? Does it mean the same thing in each stanza?

4. How do these specific uses of language embellish the basic poetic structure? How do they link stanzas, develop themes, or otherwise add meaning to stanzas?

5. Why does the last line stand alone?

6. How has the boy changed by the end? Why is this brief, seemingly trivial experience so important? How does the structure of the poem communicate the importance of this experience?

I asked students to read the poem with a partner and consider the questions I provided, then we discussed their findings as a class. They identified the obvious: four stanzas of five lines, the repetition of "I was fifteen" in each, and noted the last "I stood there, fifteen" hanging at the end. By identifying the stanzas as the underlying structure in the poem, they had already begun to structurally analyze the poem. Our task was to bring meanings into the open by looking more closely, learning how to identify both the surface and deep structures to construct meaning.

Several students fumed about the inverted word order in the first stanza. They understood that this stanza established the setting, but wanted to know why it should be made more difficult by inverting the linguistic structure. "Why can't he [Stafford] just say it?" Mary complained. "Why did he make it harder for us to understand?"

"Good question. How would you 'just say' that sentence?" I asked. We identified the main parts of speech (which turned into a minilesson on grammar) and settled on something like "I found a motorcycle (in) back of the willows one summer morning. . . ." They felt it was necessary to add the preposition "in" so the sentence made sense; we talked about why the poet might have omitted it. When the words are rearranged into "normal" speech, the caesura, or pause, before and after the words "a motorcycle" was lost. I read the stanza aloud again, so they could hear how the inversion draws attention to the motorcycle, defining it as the central image in the stanza. That the boy is fifteen, in this stanza, is a simple description of character.

Stanza two extends the metaphoric structure of the motorcycle, linking it to the first stanza. It develops a "pulsing gleam," has "shiny flanks" and "headlights fringed," becoming a "companion, ready and friendly." I asked the class what the words "flanks" and "gleam" and "fringed" meant, and I recorded the various definitions they volunteered on the chalkboard. Then we looked them up in the dictionary, but found several different definitions. Which one was right? They had to consider the context, or underlying structure of the piece, as they decided which definition "denoted" the meaning to make sense in the surface structure. "It's like the motorcycle is alive," said Danielle. "It's a horse!" But the stanzas are also linked through the system of repetition created by the lines "I was fifteen." Why are those lines repeated? Students were still curious about this particular linguistic pattern. It turned out there were two linguistic structures we were examining in this stanza. One was the image of the motorcycle, the other was the repetition of "I was fifteen."

In stanza three, the first word, "We," links the speaker and the motorcycle, and, consequently, both of the structures we examined in stanza two. ("All that in one word," I mused.) The "confident opinion" and "forward feeling" of the motorcycle reinforce this connection, extending the metaphoric motorcycle as a living thing, a companion, from stanza two to stanza three. The boy and the motorcycle anticipate springing forward, taking off to "meet the sky," a new sense of freedom that comes with being mobile and old enough to enjoy it. He is ready to take off, literally on a motorcycle, and figuratively as he comes closer to adulthood.

Reality hits in stanza four, however. The single word, "Thinking," at the very beginning is enough to bring the "forward feeling" to a crashing halt ("All that in one word!" Ryan teased). The comma after "Thinking" emphasizes the importance of the word. The metaphor of the motorcycle as companion is abruptly cut off, just as the boy snaps out of his daydream. The boy regains his senses, the owner comes into the picture, the motorcycle is back to a "machine," and the moment is over. The sharpness of the change is emphasized by the extended metaphor through the first three stanzas; in one word, "Thinking," all of the anticipation, tension, and joy created through the metaphoric structure is gone. The owner calls the boy a "good man." The irony of this is that really he is neither. He briefly considered taking the motorcycle instead of looking for an injured rider (which is not necessarily good), and he's only fifteen (which is not necessarily a man). This ironic structure further sharpens the change in mood, and as the man roars away, he leaves a dejected boy behind him. The variance of "I stood there, fifteen" as the only line that stands alone as a stanza emphasizes the loneliness and frustration of being fifteen. He is neither a man nor a child, dreaming of bigger places but left behind to just stand there, alone.

The repetition leads the reader to revise what that phrase means—retrospectively. Consciously using an objective approach means focusing on how the structure of the poem directs this revision. As the systems work with one another, tension and suspense build: Will the boy take the motorcycle, discovering what he perceives as the exciting world of chance, change, and responsibility inhabited by adults? When the boy stops to think, and searches for the owner to give the motorcycle back, the reader is left standing alone with him as the thrill of excitement and discovery is gone. Modeling a close reading of the poem helped students recognize both the surface and deep levels of meaning and begin to think about the systems at work in anything they read.

J. R. R. Tolkien's *The Hobbit*

I used *The Hobbit* to teach objective theory because it's an engaging and relatively quick book to read, and provided some interesting discussion about the transition from archetypal criticism to structural theory. First, I identified linguistic and metaphorical structures within the novel, and gave students a choice of specific structural elements to investigate as they read (Figure 3–2). I formed students into literature circles during the reading, not based on reading level, but comprised of those I felt could work well together and complement each other's learning styles. Each circle centered on one structural element. I required students to keep a reading log and write a brief description of their contribution and response to their group meetings as a means of assessing their reading progress and class work. I did not give specific quizzes, but collected the responses on a daily basis.

I was a little nervous about this project, though, because I had identified the structural elements for investigation without their input. I thought it would be better to establish a purpose for their reading rather than waiting until after they had finished reading and then brainstorm structural themes together. In doing so, I was modeling the process of identifying structural elements of storytelling within the novel which, even though these were specific only to *The Hobbit*, could be generalized to other works. Since I included other genres and activities that encouraged an objective approach throughout the unit, I felt there was more to be gained in such guided practice than in having students locate structural elements on their own. In this way, students could focus on how this helped them construct meaning rather than on what to locate within the text.

I found the literature circle format worked well; while they read and discussed in class, I worked the room, coaching them on how to examine their specific structural pattern and its development through the novel. The Narrator group, for example, found that the narrator's personal comments throughout the novel are enclosed in parentheses, and that the

The Hobbit: The Structure of "There and Back Again"

Each of you will be assigned one of the following structures to examine and chart throughout the novel. Pretend you are a scientist carefully dissecting this work; examine details carefully. Look at *words* and their definitions, the *language* of the text and what it tells you about your structure. Look at *events* associated with your structure and where they are placed in the novel. In each instance, think of the literary conventions each structure relies upon or is a part of. Remember, it is your job to make the implicit structure or convention easy for your audience to see.

1. The Role of the Narrator—What does he add to the story? At what times does he appear? Is there a pattern? Does he always say the same kinds of thing? What is the purpose of his interjections? What information does he give? Look at the punctuation of and the meaning of his comments.

2. The Hero Narrative Cycle—How does *The Hobbit* fit into this plot design? How does this plot design form a basis for other elements of characterization, metaphor, irony? Identify the "bare bones" of the narrative and evaluate them as the infrastructure for the novel.

3. The Poetry and Songs—What is the purpose of the poetry within the framework of the story? What does it add? When does it appear? Is there a pattern? What does each particular poem mean and what does it add to the section of the novel in which it is placed. Look for rhyme and repetition, metaphor and irony. Are all the poems the same? Why or why not? Is the poetry an essential element of the story?

4. Character Development of Bilbo and Dwarves—Describe and give examples of the dwarves and their behavior at the beginning of the story. Do the same for Bilbo. Continue to document and compare the development of the dwarves and Bilbo throughout the novel, carefully examining their words and actions. Do you notice a system developing? How does the behavior of each character change during the course of the novel? How do they influence one another?

5. Gandolf's Appearances and Disappearances—When does he show up? When does he disappear? What important things does he do and say? Is there a system developing for his timely arrivals and departures? What purpose does he serve?

Figure 3–2   *The Hobbit*: The Structure of "There and Back Again"

number of these comments dwindles as the novel progresses. This detail was important as they investigated whether they found the narrator to be reliable. The poetry group looked at repetitive words and phrases, the rhyme scheme and meter of each poem, and the ways in which the poetry provided characterization or background information. The Bilbo group charted his "self talk" as he longs for home as opposed to his actions in saving the dwarves time and again. The Gandalf group measured Gandalf's appearances and disappearances and discovered that each time he disappeared Bilbo took over for him with ever-increasing degrees of success. But these insights didn't come easily. The groups spent several class sessions reading and puzzling through the relevance of both objective theory and the specific structural heuristic they were given. My role as coach kept me very busy as I circulated the room.

For example, on the first day I sat with the Poetry group as they worried about the magnitude of this assignment. "We have the hardest one," they complained. "We don't even know what to do."

"What do you have to do first?" I asked. They thought for a minute, "Read the book," someone muttered.

"And while you're reading, what are you looking for?"

"Poetry," they answered, unenthusiastically.

"And when you find some poetry . . . ?" I prodded.

"We look at it to see how it fits in the story."

"Yes," I answered, "but also how each poem is structurally different or similar compared to the others in the book. Remember, if you assume an objective approach, all language in the book is important. So you should think about why the poem is placed at that particular spot in the book. How does it function?"

They wrote down a few notes and looked at me dubiously. "We have to do all the poetry?" "Well, if you are looking at how it all fits together. . . ." I shrugged and moved on to the Gandalf group.

"We've got the hardest one!" they lamented as I sat down.

While we spent much of our classroom time on small-group discussions such as this one, class discussions revolved around the difficulties and benefits of using this method. For example, one day at the beginning of class I asked them to take a few minutes to write about the strengths and weaknesses of this approach. Then we discussed their thoughts. Kyle wrote that structuralism "gets the opinion out of it. It sets down standards that make you draw off only what you see in the text." Many other students echoed his perspective. But some students, like Betsy, felt strongly that "its weakness is that it is hard to figure out the one meaning and that it might not mean what the author intended." By discussing objectivism itself, students could get their minds around this as a reading strategy, thinking about how they were constructing meaning from the words on the page. Students directed classroom discussion with their own questions and ideas about the importance of specific language and signification within the story.

In the end, each group presented its structural interpretation to the class and argued for its relevance within the basic plot structure. They were also required to turn in a written abstract of their presentation to me. They used visual aids to highlight the importance of the structure within the context of the plot, and included examples from the text to exemplify the linguistic patterns for each structure. Students created their own diagram, chart, or graph of the structural element they uncovered, representing the abstract nature of literature and language in a concrete visual form.

The first group to present was the Poetry group, who had been working in secret for a week, borrowing all of my markers, scissors, and glue, then disappearing into the back room of the library. They unveiled a huge mural on roll paper, illustrating Bilbo's journey. Curious arrangements of numbers and drawings represented the poetry that formed part of the narrative. The group's abstract summarized their ideas: "We found that the poetry in the novel introduces character, describes character, and provides background for the reader." They pointed to the first poem, describing the basic ballad structure and the story it tells. Then they moved to the poetry of the elves, goblins, and other characters. They ended with a discussion of language. "The poetry adds information that would otherwise be written into the story and would take a long time to read. The novel would not be the same without the poetry because we wouldn't know as much about the characters, not just because of what they say, but the way they say it." In other words, these students found that the poetry enhances the novel's basic plot structure. Looking closely at the structure of each poem had indeed given them a way to discover the function of poetry in the novel.

The Gandalf group developed a bar graph with Gandalf's level of activity in blue and Bilbo's in red. The x-axis along the bottom marked each chapter, and the y-axis on the side noted degree of activity based on a numerical scale they devised to measure the "presence" of each character. The section of the graph that represented the first chapters showed a high level of blue bars to represent Gandalf's presence but, as the story unfolds, a pattern began to develop. The last chapters on the graph included a high level of red. "When Gandalf is gone, Bilbo takes over," students wrote. "Gandalf's disappearance forces Bilbo to do something in an emergency. Pretty soon, he doesn't really need Gandalf to do what he needs to do. If this structure was gone from the story, Bilbo never really would have become the hero, because Gandalf still would have done everything. . . . The words Gandalf says are hints that Bilbo will be strong enough and by the end he is." The surface structure of Gandalf and Bilbo's relationship enhances the deeper structure of the heroic narrative. It was interesting to observe students using the heroic structure that we studied in the archetypal unit to comprehend the text in a different way. Matt, a member of the Gandalf group, wrote about it this way: "Mirkwood to an archetypal critic has a heavy, unconscious meaning. It represents Bilbo's unconscious mind and the spiders are the fears he must overcome. To a structuralist, the forest is just another obstacle for Bilbo to overcome on his adventure. You can't compare it to forests in other stories."

I was hopeful at the beginning of this project that students would get something out of assuming a structural stance in approaching *The Hobbit*, and they certainly did. Once again, I learned at least as much as they did, not only about the use of structural theory in constructing meaning, but also about having faith in my students as learners. They were developing more confidence in their ability to determine meaning from text, asking some good questions that reflected engaged reading, and starting discussion on their own more often.

Oedipus Rex

Because objective approaches to interpretation hearken back to Aristotle's discussion of dramatic unity in *Poetics*, I began *Oedipus Rex* with an introduction to Aristotle's theories on the structure of tragedy as he presented them (Figure 3–3). I wanted them to see that objectivist theory was not just a modern phenomenon and that Aristotle first identified an underlying dramatic structure. He argued that literary conventions like irony and symbolism were essential in embellishing that structure. According to Aristotle, the events of a perfect tragedy should unfold in a compressed time frame and limit the use of dialogue, action, and props to only what is absolutely necessary to further the plot. *Oedipus Rex* is very tightly wrought; the action takes place in one day, emphasizing the power of events. Flashback and foreshadowing; pacing of dialogue and choral commentary and odes; the prologue; episodes; and exodus all provide a clear dramatic structure. The power of tragedy becomes the swiftness of its unfolding.

Markus, a bright student who was usually quite apathetic when it came to class activities and readings, observed, "If the denotation of words is so important in being objective, we can't say we're really using this because we're not reading things in the right language. We don't know what the real words mean." He was right, we were actually reading and evaluating an entirely different linguistic structure than the original. I had to think about that for a minute. I was impressed not only that

The Structure of Tragedy

The historic philosopher from Ancient Greece, Aristotle, wrote *Poetics*, the first essay on literary criticism. In the essay, he outlined specific methods for evaluating drama and poetry, describing the basic characteristics we still use for literary interpretation. His ideas established structure in literature as the basis for interpretation and evaluation, and clearly illustrate the two levels of structure we discussed with *The Hobbit.*

The Basic Structure of Tragedy

Aristotle first developed an outline for the underlying structure of a good drama. Each of the dramatic elements listed creates the bottom layer of the structure, reinforcing dramatic unity and drawing the play onward. A good drama includes:

1. Prologue: First Act (establishing basic situation)
2. Parados: Entrance of Chorus (introducing chorus and providing background)
3. Episodes: Acts (delivering the action of the drama)
4. Stasima: Choral odes (offering the people's views, providing missing information)
5. Exodus: (providing resolution for conflict, delivering cathartic ending)

The chorus is an important structural element. The choral odes relieve tension between episodes, give background of preceding events, converse with and give advice to characters, and help the audience to interpret events.

Art Imitates Life

The surface structure in tragedy should complement the underlying plot structure. Tragedy compacts many of life's truths into a single, unified action. In other words, the tragedy should have as little extraneous detail as possible, focusing on the "truths" communicated by the systems of the work. So a good tragedy includes only the language and interaction necessary to communicate the basic truths important to the play. Yet the language is embellished with artistic ornament, challenging the audience or reader to see the situation as fresh or new.

The main character must be well structured, basically good, believable, and consistent, for the audience or reader to be horrified by his or her fate. The audience must identify with the main character and find something likeable about him or her. But the character must have some personality error or flaw that leads to a downfall.

The tragic hero's downfall arouses in the audience the emotions of pity and terror, resulting in a *catharsis* of these emotions. The audience is horrified by the end, yet

continued

Figure 3–3   The Structure of Tragedy

relieved that this is only an imitation of reality. This mixture of emotions, pity, fear, horror, and relief, provides the impact of tragedy. The work is cathartic because it purges the audience of these emotions in a safe environment. Then, relieved and cleansed, the audience can go home.

Catharsis isn't produced by violent actions, however. In the ancient tragedies, violence doesn't take place before the audience—reports of violence are given, but not enacted. Too much violence detracts from the basic plot.

The Tragic Hero

Aristotle defined the concept of the tragic hero. The irony of tragedy lies in the contrast between the vision which the tragic hero has of his future and the shocking disaster that befalls him. The structure of this irony traces the descent of the hero; the individual's suffering refines him or her, causing a deeper understanding of the condition of man. Again, the audience understands this irony as a mixture of pity for and revulsion at the character (or catharsis).

The tragic hero begins the story with supreme pride and confidence in his own freedom. But the hero has an enormous capacity for suffering as he further develops throughout the play. He exhibits a sense of commitment to his cause, and vigorously protests forces working against him.

Thought Questions

1. Are Aristotle's methods still practiced today? When have you experienced catharsis as you finished a book or watched a movie?
2. How has modern drama evolved from Aristotle's ancient tragedies? Consider in particular the question of violence and the unity of time, place, and action.
3. If art imitates life, how appropriate are the differences in ancient Greek tragedy and modern American tragedy? What "life" is each imitating?

Figure 3–3 *continued*

he had made such a cognitive leap, but that he had contributed to discussion on his own accord. I asked the rest of the students what they thought, and they decided that we were still learning something useful if we practiced applying objective interpretation on translations like *Oedipus Rex*.

Understanding the concepts of "ironic structure" ("Ionic what?" asked one student) and dramatic irony was the basic challenge in an objective analysis of the play. Irony in any work (movies included) creates tension and suspense while provoking laughter and tears. A thread of irony can weave its way through a work, wrapping up all characters and events in the end, creating a structure of its own through language and events. The dramatic structure of *Oedipus* is embellished by many ironies: the eye imagery in Oedipus' dialogue; the wisdom of Teiresias; Oedipus' blind anger; Jocasta's diversionary tactics; and Oedipus' curse on the one who killed King Laius at the onset of the play. Irony helps to establish character and drive the play forward.

The textbook version of the play was not exceedingly difficult reading, and we read some of the play together as a class, some in the dramatic irony groups, and some I assigned as homework. Class discussion centered on the ironies of the drama, and the merits of Aristotelian theory (students rolled that term around in their mouths like a jawbreaker; "A-ris-toe-TEEL-ian" turned out to be fun to say) as a means to construct meaning from the minimal dialogue and the swift turn of events. This helped them come to terms with some parts of the play they felt were hard to swallow. "There's no way Jocasta doesn't know who he really is," they argued. "How can someone miss the scars on his feet, and the fact that he showed up just after Laius disappeared? Didn't they ever talk about the fact that he actually killed someone on his way there?" But they couldn't wait to enact some of the scenes from the play in their dramatic reading (Figure 3–4).

Irrepressible teenage humor manifested itself once again through the dramatic projects (maybe that's one reason I like doing these so much). In one, Amy played Aristotle by sticking cottonballs on her face with petroleum jelly to resemble a beard. "He's like Gandalf," she explained, "because he's kind of a guide." We watched them fall off, one by one, every time she spoke. In another presentation, Ryan plunged brooches (taken from his mother's jewelry box) into eyeballs made with strategically decorated raw eggs, creating a huge mess, but also a huge impact on his audience (it truly was cathartic!). There was the solemn group in full costume with candles and flowing robes, and the wacky group that, for some reason, presented Oedipus galloping across the stage with reindeer antlers on his head. But they fulfilled the criteria I had specified in the guidelines for the presentation, and could respond to the class questions when they were finished, so I considered the exercise a success.

Contemplating the tragic hero and the nature of Oedipus' tragic flaw brought us back to archetypal theory. Students wondered if catharsis could really be an objective concept, because it is based on the experience a reader or member of the audience has with the work. I explained that catharsis was built by the irony of the play, that irony "set up" the audience to fully experience the catharsis of Oedipus' self-mutilation, so it was actually an objective concept. For effect, I shared the Roman philosopher Seneca's version of the blinding of Oedipus. Seneca vividly describes how Oedipus rips his eyeballs out with his bare hands instead

Dramatic Reading and *Oedipus Rex*

For this project, we will read the play *Oedipus Rex*, by ancient Greek dramatist Sophocles, together in class, applying Aristotle's views on tragedy and the tragic hero, examining the structural layers of the play. We will be using both the basic underlying dramatic structure as identified by Aristotle and the irony created by the language of the play as a basis for interpreting structures. You will be assigned to a group that will focus on one within the play.

We will focus on five major structural elements present in the play:

The Abuse of Power: Is Oedipus' cause noble, or is he abusing his position? Who else has power in the play?

Human Will versus Fate: Is the disaster inevitable? Who could have stopped it?

Nature of Tragic Hero: Is Oedipus worthy of our concern or sympathy?

Nature of Responsibility: Who behaves responsibly, or irresponsibly? How does this contribute to the catastrophe at the end?

The Nature of Justice: Who is guilty? Who is innocent? Has justice been served at the end?

Choose one of these structural concepts and examine the play for the following information:

- At what point in the play does it become present? How does it fit in the structure of the drama?
- How does it contribute to Oedipus' eventual downfall? Look for irony. Note ironic passages in the dialogue and language of the play. How does irony function to build tension and suspense?
- How does it fit into Aristotle's views of tragedy?
- Identify and discuss the structural irony of your concept. How does the play's irony make the theme more striking? Cite specific passages.

As a group, you will prepare to present your findings on and reaction to your particular theme as it is apparent in the play. This presentation must:

- Include dramatized (live) examples from the play that exemplify the development and importance of the concept. Dialogue choices should reflect irony.
- Discuss the ironic structure of your concept, emphasizing the creation of tension and suspense leading to a cathartic ending. This should focus on the upper level structure of language and embellishment.
- Commentary on the development of your concept from an "Aristotelian" viewpoint, explaining how it fits into his structural theories. This should highlight the importance of a basic underlying layer of dramatic structure in events of the play.

Your presentation should last about fifteen minutes and each participant in your group should have equal speaking time. Include costumes and props, but you do not need to memorize lines; use notecards instead.

Figure 3–4   Dramatic Reading and *Oedipus Rex*

of using brooches to stab out his eyes, a satisfying "gross-out" for students. We talked about who had responsibility for what in the play, and the discussion turned to how people don't want to take responsibility for their actions in today's society. Students brought up current events as evidence that ironies run throughout our lives, and art does indeed mirror life. They pondered abuses of power present in the news and in the daily routine of school. Who has power in our culture, and how is it used or abused? Do human beings control events through sheer will, or does Fate decide much of what happens in our lives? Ryan brought up the common "insanity" defense often used in criminal trials, Sheri pondered the implications of "political correctness" on individual responsibility, Matt referred to events from *The Jerry Springer Show* and how the people who appear on it never take responsibility for their actions. I silently considered the irony of this discussion of personal responsibility taking place in a classroom full of adolescents.

Further Teaching Ideas

- Frame stories (*The Canterbury Tales*, the *Decameron*, or *A Thousand and One Nights*) are excellent vehicles for examining layers of language and meaning.

- Have students structurally analyze their own writing using the myths they wrote in the archetypal unit. Using the myths also shows how a different approach yields different interpretive results.

- Examine the language of Instant Messaging (IM) or the structure of websites to introduce or review an objective approach to constructing meaning from text. What are the conventions that direct the way language is used in online, synchronous (IM), or asynchronous (email messages or weblog postings) communications?

More Readings for Teaching Objective Theory

The Inferno by Dante Alighieri

Monster by Walter Dean Myers

ttyl (Talk to You Later) by Lauren Myracle, a YA novel written entirely in IM form.

4 *Segments and Gaps: Teaching Students Reader-Response Theory*

Identity defines what the individual brings from old experiences to new ones . . . Interpretation is a function of identity.

—Norman Holland

Teaching response theory encouraged students to become cognizant of how they construct meaning, and served as an extension of reading strategy instruction. This is much more than asking students how a reading made them feel; in fact, I found that explicitly teaching response theory offered students much more structure than I had initially envisioned. In recent years, response theory has become nearly transparent as an underlying assumption for many student-centered teaching practices. But many teachers aren't aware of the ways in which this informs their practice, and don't openly discuss theory with students as a reading or interpretive method. In systematically teaching response theory in this four-week unit, I didn't have to significantly change my teaching practice. The difference was that this time I shared the underlying theory for using these methods with students, making implicit beliefs and expectations explicit. I hoped to stretch the concept of "reading strategy" to "interpretive strategy" by situating response theory in the larger field of literary theory. It is important, however, to clarify exactly what response theory is, and what it is not, to fully explore how it can be presented as an approach to understanding text.

Essentials of Reader-Response Theory

Reader-response theory assumes that a text cannot be understood apart from the response it elicits from the reader because it is the emotional and intellectual response of the reader that gives the text meaning in the first place. I relied on the research of response theorists Louise Rosenblatt, Wolfgang Iser, and Stanley Fish to identify the processes of response interpretation for students in a methodical and evaluative way. These scholars have been influential in establishing and continuing research in the field of reader-response pedagogy through their perspectives on the ways in which a reader's response informs a construction of meaning, inspiring a generation of educators to continue developing student-centered teaching practices.

The work of Louise Rosenblatt emphasizes the ways in which students should validate their initial interpretation of a work. Rosenblatt first wrote on the subject in 1937 and is the forerunner in the reader-response field, even though her work wasn't generally accepted until the 1970s. Rosenblatt argued that the "text" exists as a transaction somewhere between the words and the reader. She wrote: "[It] is hard to liberate ourselves from the notion that the poem is something either entirely mental or entirely external to readers. 'The poem' cannot be equated solely with either the text or the experience of a reader. . . . 'poem' is understood to refer to the relationship between a reader and a text" (105). Each reading of a text is an "event" that will never be exactly the same again, even if the same reader reads the same text. She further argued that "the priority of the lived-through relationship with the text should be maintained. Anything, any knowledge, that may help us to such participation is to be valued. With that clearly in mind, we can welcome any 'background knowledge' that may enhance our ability to validly organize the experience generated by the text . . ." (1994, 125). By using the word "validly" to describe the interpretative process, Rosenblatt emphasizes that not just any personal associations or interpretations are acceptable, but there must be some validity to those associations. This is essential to understand response theory, and I relied heavily on this concept with students throughout the unit.

The research of German critic Wolfgang Iser helped students conceive of how they read and respond to the words on the page. Iser believes that the act of reading is complex; that we can do it at all constitutes a phenomenon. Calling his study of the process "phenomenology," he explains the act of reading as "a product arising out of the interaction between text and reader," an interaction between the structure of the text and its recipient, and argues that a text consists of a series of segments, or "instructions," the reader uses to construct a framework of meaning. However, Iser places an emphasis on "gaps" in the text, describing them as "the fundamental asymmetry between text and reader, that give[s] rise to communication in the reading process" (Keesey 1987, 149). The text as it stands on the page is incomplete, it is simply a set of instructions for creating an imaginative work within the mind of the reader. This indeterminacy, however, "stimulates the reader into filling the blanks with projections. He is drawn into the events and made to supply what is meant from what is not said . . . it is the implications and not the statements that give shape and weight to the meaning. But as the unsaid comes to life in the reader's imagination, so the said 'expands' to take on greater significance . . . what is concealed spurs the reader into actions, but this action is also controlled by what is revealed" (Keesey 1987, 149). "Whatever is present is marked by an absence . . . the task of interpretation is thus dual in nature . . . the absent and the present are made continually to point at each other" (Iser 2000, 72). He argues, like Rosenblatt, that the "real" text is an imaginative, fluid entity existing somewhere between the reader's expectations and the words on the page, although textual constraints drive a reader's interpretation.

Theorist Stanley Fish's concept of interpretive communities helped students recognize the importance of a social reaction to the text and the role of discussion in determining a final interpretation. Despite the uniqueness of individuals, cultural and social values strongly influence individual readings; readers who have cultural or social similarities will read texts with a comparable response because their life experiences have been very similar. "Meanings are the property . . . of interpretive communities that are responsible both for the shape of a reader's activities and for the texts those activities produce" (Fish 1999, 268). In other words, members of the same interpretive community (World Literature class, in this case) tend to rely on similar reading strategies and produce similar readings because they have a shared experience of reading the same text. The gaps Iser describes are filled as the class engages in posing and answering questions and students make similar associations with the work. Then discussion allows students to explore each other's background knowledge within an interpretive framework and test the validity of the resulting interpretations.

Response Theory as Reading Strategy

In essence, response theory calls attention to how we read and what influences our reading, and seeks both to define the act of reading itself, and to identify the processes a reader must go through to construct a meaning from a given text. Consequently, a literary work is not defined by the words on the page, but as a transaction between text and reader as the reader processes those words. The reader becomes engaged with a work, making a personal connection with the events, characters, theme, and/or setting. This connection can come from prior knowledge through personal experience, cultural associations, and previous literary experience. Focusing on textual structure, the background of the author or the historical relevance of the setting may initially provide specific interpretive resources for both teacher and student, but, according to response theorists, these approaches only serve to direct, not replace or supersede, the essential prior knowledge or experiential background that informs reading a text.

I had often struggled with response-based practice, as I indicated in the last chapter, because I didn't know how to draw the line between an off-the-cuff response and one that was sincere. But when I reread Rosenblatt, Iser, and Fish carefully so I could teach the approach, I realized that response theory did not mean accepting random interpretations from inexperienced readers. Unfortunately, response theorists are sometimes faced with charges of relativism by those who advocate more objective approaches to literary interpretation, or who are not well versed in the actual work of the scholars in the field. *Relativism* is the term for the belief that there are as many ways of constructing a meaning of any text as there are individuals who read it, and no reader's response can ever be completely wrong. This is not response theory; accepting anything as interpretive undermines the value of literature, because if all writing or communication can mean whatever anyone wants it to mean, then the craft of writing and skill in making an argument both become irrelevant and the text itself is rendered meaningless. In reality, reader-response theory is neither relative nor objective but instead views the text and reader as interdependent; readers orchestrate interpretive strategies, using everything they know to construct meaning from text. Response as an interpretive literary approach does not legitimize a random flow of readers' affective experiences and call those ideas literary interpretation. Response theorists seek not to accept any response, but to identify the strategies a reader uses to construct meaning, isolate specific elements of this process, and explore the basic question of how a reader constructs meaning from a text.

Essentially, then, explicitly teaching response theory is very similar to explicitly teaching reading strategies. The goal is to have students think about how they are thinking, how they are creating a relationship with and eliciting meaning from the text, and how the text might support differing interpretations. To do this, students should develop the skills that enable them to recognize the signals communicated by the text and to discover how they, as readers, are interpreting those signals. Specific information on reader-response theories of reading and literary interpretation can help them become more objective about being affective. Explicitly sharing these concepts with students encourages "responsible" associations without accepting almost anything they choose to blurt out during discussion. Students can understand how a text evokes an emotional response from the reader, how the work is shaped by interaction between the reader and the text, and how the reader must orchestrate interpretive strategies to construct meaning. They can come to understand what they are doing when they read and respond to a text, how they should be held accountable for their interpretations, and how discussion helps a reader clarify and revise that interpretation. If this sounds very similar to the goals I set for teaching literary theory in general, it's because asking students to construct meaning from text in any form is asking them to generate and articulate a response. Assuming a response perspective becomes another way to externalize the cognitive mysteries of reading and literary interpretation.

Teaching Reader-Response Theory

I began by giving a general overview of response theory, using a handout to guide discussion (Figure 4–1). The thought questions were designed to activate students' prior knowledge of the ways experience and associations can drive interpretation and response and also to demonstrate how meaning lies somewhere between "fact" and perception. When two people tell the same story, their versions are usually somewhat different because they focus on different details. The meaning of favorite childhood cartoons viewed from an adult (or adolescent) perspective might change as additional prior knowledge of society helps the viewer pick up on adult allusions, references, and jokes (think Bugs Bunny).

"So why can't we answer a question right?" one student wondered. "When we have to answer a teacher's question, or one in the book, isn't it just what they think some story means? If I say something different, why are they right and I'm wrong?"

"You shouldn't always be wrong if you've carefully read the story," I responded. "But it's important to have experience with literature and reading, too, and teachers usually have more experience in understanding the ways in which a story is told. Those kinds of questions are usually designed to help you clarify the problems you might have in understanding a story, like identifying main ideas or learning new vocabulary. Remember, you can't just ignore the information the text gives you; response theory doesn't say 'anything goes.' But knowing about literary theory and reading new material helps you get that experience instead of relying on mine, or a textbook's, all the time. Then you can ask your own questions when you read."

Modeling Response Theory and the Reading Process

Next, we explored ways to practice response theory as an interpretive method. I designed a Reader-Response Concept Map (Figure 4–2) using concepts from Iser, Rosenblatt, and Fish to define what I was talking about when I referred to the "reading process." I described the process in three steps: (1) Iser's theory illustrates what readers do (or should do) in their head as they read, (2) Rosenblatt's identifies how a reader might decide a meaning is valid, and (3) Fish explores the "social" reaction to

Reader-Response Theory

The act of reading is amazing, when you really think about it. How do we make sense of the little black squiggles on a page, turning them into elaborate stories and ideas? Reader-response theorists explore the reading process and the ways we create meaning from a jumble of letters and words on a page.

As we read, we take in the information given to us by the words on the page, but we also "plug in" our personal associations with the characters and situations in a story. Our experiences in life and with literature provide the context for creating a version of the story in our minds. In other words, we turn the words on the page into mental images *ourselves* by filling in our own experience, and the version of the story in our minds becomes different from the printed version in our hands.

But our versions can't be too different from the text; there is a give and take going on between the text and the reader that response theorists call "transaction." We continually update and revise our version of the story when we get new information from the text (by reading another paragraph or chapter), talk about it with someone else (class discussion and literature circles), or mature and go back and read the same story again.

Because this approach focuses on the *reader's response* and the *process* of creating meaning using the cues given by the text, it is acceptable for readers with different life experiences and expectations for a work to interpret characters and events differently, even though the words in the story are the same. After all, the reader's mind transacts with the text to create meaning; how can two interpretations be exactly the same? Should they be?

Thinking About Response Theory

1. Think back to a memorable experience that you had that involved several other people. When you tell about the experience, do you tell the story in the same way as the other people who were with you? How are they similar? How are they different? Why do you think there are any differences?
2. Think back to a favorite story, movie, or TV show from your childhood. Watch the movie or show, or read the book again. How is it different to you now? Is your imaginative creation different than it was before? Do you know more about the circumstances or catch more of the jokes now? How do you explain this?

Figure 4–1   Reader-Response Theory

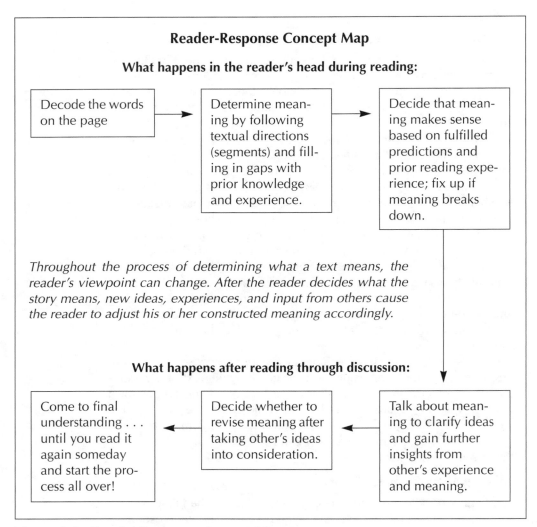

Figure 4–2   Reader-Response Concept Map

the text and the importance of talking about what we read to clarify that meaning. I explained who these theorists were and what they thought; students were interested and valued knowing the inside story about how they may have learned not only to interpret literature in past classes, but more about how they had learned to read in the first place.

I modeled the steps on the concept map by conducting a think-aloud. I didn't go into too much detail about filling in gaps and determining meaning the first time around, but used the think-aloud as a review of reading strategy instruction they may have had in previous classes. I used "20/20" by Linda Brewer (1996), a piece of microfiction, but just about anything would work for modeling: short poetry, news briefs, quotations, excerpts of song lyrics, even product labels or advertisements. I placed a copy of the text I was using on the overhead, saying, "First, I need to decode the words," and read the story aloud once (box one on the concept map). Then, using an overhead marker, I read it again, this time underlining words and phrases that gave me information, thinking aloud about how I understood the details so far. For example, I identified familiar words, described associations and experiences the text called up for me, talked about what I knew about the way stories are told, and how all these things helped me to understand this one. "But I have some questions," I said, "about things that aren't clear; these are gaps in my understanding of the meaning." I circled these with a marker in a different color. I continued to pose questions I had about the details aloud, and looked to the details I had previously identified given by the text to help me fill them in (box two on the concept map). Finally, I said, "I think this is about . . ." and decided on what I thought the story meant (box three). I then opened the floor for discussion by saying, "I still have some questions. I need to hear your thoughts to help me clarify this meaning" (box four), and took student comments to help me do so. I made some revisions based on their comments and the discussion that ensued, and we decided together what the story meant. Well, sort of. At this point, students were pretty much following my lead, but that's the point of modeling as an instructional method.

Applying Reader-Response Theory

By conducting a think-aloud, I learned that further exploration of Iser's "segments and gaps" helped students understand that the text drives interpretive response, not the other way around. We further explored this concept by keeping a Segments/Gaps Record (Figures 4–3a, 4–3b). Segments can be recognized as the framework of a text: the title, paragraphs, sentences, images, syntactical units or individual words, depending upon the level of analysis the text requires. Yet between each segment is a gap that the reader must fill in with experiences or knowledge in order to make sense of the text. The reader goes back and forth between personal response and the text, sorting through the meaning of a given segment, filling in the gaps with personal feelings, associations, or experiences to make sense of the segment, finding a logical, thematic connection from one segment to the next. Throughout this process, the reader predicts, confirms, reviews, and adapts the meaning of segments,

Segments/Gaps Record Text

Response critics are interested in the mental picture or intellectual re-creation of the text that each reader constructs in the process of reading. The text (story, poem, or novel) gives the reader "instructions" on creating that mental picture by describing the character and setting, presenting a series of events, maintaining point of view, etc. Wolfgang Iser, a German literary critic, calls those instructions *segments*. The segments are the concrete descriptions and details that are consistent; they are specifically given to the reader.

If a character in a work is described as mean and nasty, or brilliant and charming, the reader accepts these given instructions on creating the character accurately and keeps them in mind. But if the story only describes the characters' actions and appearance instead of giving clear instructions, there is a *gap* the reader must fill in mentally constructing the character. Iser believes readers make sense of the gaps, or omission of detail, by filling them in with their own experiences they associate with the information given.

So, if a character is described as nosy and talkative, some readers can interpret the character as annoying because they have a nosy and talkative little sister who can drive them crazy. Another reader, who enjoys baby-sitting for a funny and adorable boy who is nosy and talkative may interpret this character as endearing. The readers have come to different interpretation of character because they have different experiences and associations with talkative people. They have filled in the gap with their experience. How will the two agree on the initial determination of character? Should they have to? Often, the reader is given further instruction on character interpretation as the story progresses, but that first impression is an important one.

To practice with identifying segments and gaps, it is helpful to record them as you read a story. If it is difficult for you to record gaps, try listing the questions you have about details in the story. If you have a question about something, there is a gap in the instructions you have been given, or you have missed some information you were given by the author. Questions can also clarify the segments, help you to verbalize the missing information, or cause you to reread a section in which meaning broke down; when you answer your questions, you are also identifying the experiences you are plugging into the gaps.

Fill in the column to record Segments as you read with details and instructions from the story. Record any questions you have about those segments in the Questions column. The questions can help you identify instructions or information that seem to be missing. Fill in the column for Gaps with either your answers to your own questions, or the information you feel is missing. Pay careful attention to *how* you are answering those questions.

Figure 4–3a   Segments/Gaps Record Text

	Segments/Gaps Record Sheet	
SEGMENTS	**QUESTIONS**	**GAPS**
1.	1.	1.
2.	2.	2.
3.	3.	3.
4.	4.	4.
5.	5.	5.
6.	6.	6.
7.	7.	7.
8.	8.	8.

Figure 4–3b   Segments/Gaps Record Sheet

all in the split second it takes to read across the page (hence the term *phenomenology*). Not only does creating the links between segments drive readers, but it also conditions readers' view of previous segments as they anticipate and predict events in the upcoming segments. Therefore readers have continually modified their viewpoint, becoming enraptured with the development and fluidity of their mental construct of the text.

Questioning activities are excellent methods to draw specific experiences out of students by highlighting the gaps; when students pose, then answer, their own questions, they are articulating the experiences they use to fill the gaps. Each successive segment is also followed by a gap that the reader must fill for that segment to make sense and connect to the next, a process that continues throughout the reader's engagement with a work. It is the implications and not the statements in a given work that draw the reader onward; this again illustrates that we read not only because of what the work gives, but also by what is withheld. Students did have some difficulty identifying how they are influenced by what is not there ("If it's not there, how can I find it?"). This is the crux of the Segments/Gaps Record. The assignment asked them to identify information that they are given and record any questions this information raised. In the process, they became more aware of the experiences they plugged into the text through the internal questioning that carried them forward as they read.

"The Lottery"

I used the short story "The Lottery," by Shirley Jackson, to further model and allow students to apply reader-response interpretation. I distributed copies of the first half of the story (I didn't give them the whole story because I wanted them to discuss their predictions and impressions before we read the ending) and put a copy of the Segments/Gaps Record on the overhead. I read the first couple of paragraphs aloud, just as I had modeled previously, and we worked together to record segments, questions, and gaps.

"The most obvious first segment of any work is the title," I said. "It is the initial instruction for the reader, but there are certainly gaps in a very short title like this one. The first question I have when I read this is, What is a lottery?" Some students volunteered positive associations with lotteries, involving the chance to win money or prizes, while some associated wasted money and false hopes with the title. I summarized their thoughts by saying, "We do know that the story somehow involves a game of chance, which can be construed as a positive or negative thing."

"Okay," I continued, "The next segments in the story are presented in the first sentence, and provide instructions on setting for the reader," and I read the sentence aloud: "The morning of June 27 was clear and sunny with the fresh warmth of a full-summer day; the flowers were blossoming profusely and the grass was richly green." Students agreed that these details emphasize positive associations with beautiful summer days, evoking calming emotions. "But what does that have to do with a lottery?" Sarah wondered. "Well, that's one of those gaps that you have to fill. We try to make a connection between the title and the first sentence in order to move on to the next segment. Does this help you decide what you think about the title or how the story is going to unfold?"

"It makes me feel like the lottery might be a good thing," offered Angie.

These good feelings were confirmed by the next segment describing school children just recently released for summer vacation, although some students zeroed in on the description of boys gathering stones. The class remembered the joy of summer days stretching endlessly before them through the cultural lens of American summertime holidays and picnics. "Doesn't everyone know a kid named Bobby like the one in the story?" asked Ashley (these may or may not be pleasant associations). "And packs of annoying boys running around, looking for trouble," added Susan. "But why are they picking up stones?" Jacob asked.

"Boys collect rocks, boys throw stones. Everyone knows that," said Susan.

"But why are they collecting them? Why are they hoarding them and keeping them from each other?" I ask. "These are gaps. We don't really know what they want to do and we have to 'fill in' or predict what we think the segments mean so far. I know that these details are there for a reason in a story."

Susan and Jacob launched into the following debate, which clearly illustrated how different readers can fill in gaps with different associations.

SUSAN: "Lotteries are stupid, just a waste of time and money. Nobody really wins anything; people who play in lotteries are pretty dumb. I don't know anyone who has ever won something like that.

JACOB: But somebody always has to win a lottery. It depends on how big it is and how many people are involved. We sell raffle tickets at church and somebody always wins the prize.

SUSAN: Yeah, the only real winners are the people who make money selling lotteries!

ME: So when you think about the title of this story, Sarah, why do you think it's important, based on your experiences with lotteries?

SUSAN: "I guess I just think these people are going to be stupid or just losers. There are always more losers in a lottery than winners. Besides, this is a small hick town. That means these people really don't have anything to win in a raffle. They probably get to win a cake or a cow.

JACOB: I think somebody will win something. It's probably money, maybe half the money of the raffle. It's the beginning of summer, so they are probably going to celebrate with a picnic or something.

Susan and Jacob's experience with lotteries led to different meanings for the title and main symbol of the story. I asked them how they knew if their experiences were helping them to logically interpret events in the story.

SUSAN: What I just told you. Lotteries are dumb; I just understand that these people are dumb.

JACOB: I think they are just following their tradition . . .

SUSAN: Which is dumb! And those boys are gonna whip those stones. Nothing good ever comes out of boys with piles of stones! I don't know, but I think something bad is going to happen.

This was quite different from the positive associations Angie expressed earlier. When I pressed Susan to explain why she thought so, she described an uneasy "feeling" she had, saying, "Lots of times in stories you just know there will be some surprise at the end." Her past experiences with literature helped her to validate her uneasiness with lotteries, stones, and the people involved.

JACOB: Maybe the boys just collect stones and don't want their friends to have more than they do. They all know each other pretty well and maybe they just do this sometimes.

This exchange illustrated how gaps create tension and suspense as a reader attempts to determine how the segments fit together. Questions about the gaps and the anticipation of upcoming segments to answer those questions draw the reader onward. The differences in answers mark the differences in the texts the readers are constructing. One reader may sense impending trouble (Boys . . . with rocks!!) while another may associate rocks with innocent collecting or building a fort. Somehow, the reader's experience with summertime, boys, and rocks must link segments together and drive the narrative forward. "How do we decide who's right?" I asked the class. "Finish the story!" Patrick answered, rolling his eyes.

I assigned the rest of the first half of the story as homework, requiring students to use the Segments/Gaps Record Sheet to note, as they read, when the text provided specific information, and when they found they had questions about significant omission of information. As "The Lottery" continues, the reader begins to pick up on the uneasiness of the townspeople who gather in the town square. Yet the relationship between this uneasiness, the summertime, the rocks, and town tradition is still unclear.

In class the next day, I refer back to the Reader-Response Concept Map. "When you read the story on your own, you went through the first three steps: decoding, segments and gaps, and determining meaning," I begin. "I'm not so sure about the last one," said Patrick. "I still don't get what is going on!"

"Today we're going to discuss that, Patrick, in small groups. Talking about what you've read with someone else might help. That's what the last three steps of the reading process are all about." Discussion tests individual interpretations, supporting or refuting each student's experienced meaning as they clarify ideas by arguing them with someone else. A community of readers serves as a sounding board for ideas and interpretations inspired by a work. In any kind of reading group members seek to understand and be understood, in other words, to have their ideas critically validated. The individual construction of the text continues to develop through discussion. "In your discussion, share the questions and answers you recorded as gaps in the story and see if you had some of the same questions."

They protested, "How can we answer them if we don't know the whole story?"

"Do the best you can" I said. "Predict if you have to. We're just comparing notes at this point." The groups discussed their questions and predictions, without coming to a clear consensus on whether the story would come to a good or bad end. I just floated from group to group, monitoring discussion and shrugging my shoulders, encouraging them to talk to one another instead of looking to me for answers. My role was to help them with questions about theory, not to interpret the story for them.

The next day the class was supposed to have finished the story, recorded more segments, gaps, and questions, and come prepared to discuss in their groups. Jacob was horrified by the ending, but Susan said, "See, I told you they were hicks from a small town and pretty stupid. Why else would they do such a crazy thing?" Susan had arrived at the conclusion that such things may happen in small backward towns where tradition and ritual can lead people to do very senseless things. Susan thought the story was meaningful and thought-provoking, because tradition itself was questionable; everyone follows traditions that don't make any sense. Jacob was reading the same words but with much different results. He associated the lottery with luck and winning, the stones and little boys meant summer fun and games, tradition brought the experience of comfort and connection to family and history, small-town-inspired visions of friendship and cooperation. To him, the ending was difficult to accept. Why would townspeople want to brutally kill a productive and loved member of their society? He couldn't quite see the point and decided he did not like the story. Both students had set up some criteria for judging the events of the story and ascribing meaning to them. Whose experience is the "correct" one?

By the end of the discussion, Jacob had allowed that sometimes tradition and ritual can seem senseless when participants lose sight of why they are engaging in the traditional act, so the ending made more sense to him. But he also influenced Susan to find the good in tradition as well. "Don't forget," he said, "that summer vacation is a tradition!" Susan conceded that ritual does have an important place in our lives, but that we should try to remember why we take part in traditional activities ("Why don't we go to school in the summer, anyway?" she wondered). Her construct of the text changed somewhat through discussion: both students clarified their own ideas and validated the other interpretation. In a way, the two agreed to disagree, a process Rosenblatt called a "criteria of adequacy" (1994, 124). Maybe they disagreed on interpretive details, but at least they could sigh that the other reader's interpretation was adequate, if not as valid as their own.

Fighting the Text: Responding to the Unfamiliar

Knowing about theory, in particular reader-response theory, was especially helpful when students were reading a text that was completely unfamiliar, or even outlandish. Works like "A Hunger Artist" by Franz Kafka or "The Very Old Man with Enormous Wings" by Gabriel García Márquez really test a student's interpretive skills. There are more gaps, and the reader must rely heavily on past literary experience or personal responses to construct meaning. Readings become variant as more of individual readers' experiences guide their particular construct, making a final determination of meaning even more complicated. Critic Terry Eagleton recognizes that Iser's emphasis on the absence in a text particularly lends itself to an appreciation of "modernist, multiple works partly because they make us more self-conscious about the labour of interpreting them . . . the reader comes to construct a working hypothesis . . . [and] is engaged in fighting the text as much as interpreting it" (1996, 70–1). But it is the idea of "fighting the text" that puts many students off; if meaning isn't clear and readily constructed, they will pronounce the work "stupid" and disregard it. I found, however, that when students knew they were filling in gaps, even unfamiliar circumstances and difficult texts were not as frustrating for them because they had purpose for "fighting the text."

Response Theory and *Hamlet*

I didn't choose to teach *Hamlet*, my students chose to read it. I had given them a choice of Shakespearean plays from the classroom sets of paperbacks stored in the English office. They chose *Hamlet* because they had "heard of it before." This was fine with me, because response theory seemed to be the ideal approach for reading about literature's most famous dysfunctional family. In our age of divorce and remarriage, family counseling, and blended families, there are few students who have not had some experience with "unique" family relationships. I was sure that Hamlet's friendship with Horatio, his confusion about his own feelings for Ophelia, his complex relationship with his mother, and his competitive and resentful feelings for Claudius would strike familiar chords and help students engage with the play in a way that was meaningful to them on a personal level.

Initially, students were intimidated by Shakespearean language and convention, and it was hard to keep myself from relieving their fears by giving them too much of my own responses in the opening scenes. But because they knew we were learning about theory at the same time that we were learning about *Hamlet*, students didn't become overly frustrated; focusing on response theory gave them a purpose for reading. We had already discussed the importance of segments, so the structural or linguistic study of the play wasn't overshadowed by personal experiences as students read. Ironically, because they were more cognitive of the ways they filled in gaps and how they participated in the construction of meaning, students more carefully examined the segments, in this case poetic language, that give the play texture and structure.

Before we began reading, however, I reviewed the Reader-Response Concept Map so they could follow the model for their individual reading and small-group discussion. Then I gave them a Response Log (Figure 4–4) to keep as a kind of journal, which was similar to the Segments/Gaps Record Sheet so they had a familiar framework for keeping track of their thoughts as they read.

I also encouraged students to "buddy up" and read with a partner so they could gain confidence by working through the language and developing a valid interpretation together. I found that, as students began to relate Hamlet and his circumstances to their own experiences and lives,

Hamlet Response Log

Reader response as a method of interpretation requires carefully identifying your response and how the text has elicited that response. Keep
a log recording specific lines, general events, and character actions
that particularly impress you, confuse you, or otherwise draw a
response. What *segments* are impressive or outstanding? What *gaps*
leave you wondering? What questions are you left with? How do you
make sense of those gaps by injecting your own experiences and associations? Keeping track of this information will help you to understand
how you are creating an individual relationship with and interpretation of the text.

Quotation, situation, event	Act, scene, line number	Importance of segment, questions about gaps	Your response to segment, answer to question

Figure 4–4   *Hamlet* Response Log

the "buddies" arrived at individual interpretations. In fact, they often argued most vehemently with one another instead of looking to me to give them the bottom line. It was more meaningful for them to pose and answer their own questions than to answer teacher- or textbook-generated questions.

Throughout the play, many of their questions centered on the characters and their relationships with one another, so I focused on that aspect of their experience by assigning an activity called "persona writing" (Figure 4–5). Students were to assume the persona of one character in the play and explore that character's motivation by writing a hypothetical letter to another character regarding a specific event or interaction. This gave students the chance to articulate and expand on their conception of different characters. One day, Ashley shared the letter she had written from Ophelia to Hamlet in which she told him she was pregnant. She had decided this was the best way to explain why Ophelia lost her wits and drowned herself, arguing that, without such extenuating circumstances, Ophelia would have known Laertes would come home and take care of her when he heard the news of their father's death. She had also gotten the idea from Kenneth Branagh's version of *Hamlet*, which includes a bedroom scene with Ophelia and Hamlet. Just as the debate about this possibility began, a couple of students from an Advanced Placement English class stopped in for a visit. They were stunned at the subject of our discussion. "No way!" one said. "She just goes mad because her father was killed. That's what the play says!"

"But what about what the play leaves out?" Ashley asked.

"If it doesn't say it, then it isn't there," the AP student shot back. The students in the other class understood the play from the objective, text-based perspective that had been translated for them by the particular anthology they used. Consequently, the visiting students believed they had learned the "real" meaning of the play. Because this World Literature course was not constrained by AP test preparation, we had more freedom to open up discussion of variant readings. Other students in the class argued in Ashley's defense and they all debated reasons for Ophelia's madness for a few minutes before the visitors left. "Good thing we had already learned about [objective theory]," said Ashley, "or I would have thought I was really dumb!"

The important point of this exchange is not the debate itself, or the subject of the debate; it is the variance in meaning construction that resulted from different interpretive communities. Quite by accident, we were able to witness evidence of how a class becomes an interpretive community and influences a student's interpretation of and response to a story. Because the interpretive community in World Literature was different from the interpretive community of Advanced Placement English,

Creating a Character
Persona Writing in *Hamlet*

The term *persona* literally refers to the mask a character wears in a literary work, or the ways in which the character is revealed through dialogue, action, and reaction. For this assignment, it is your job to assume the persona of a character from *Hamlet* to make some judgments about what is going on behind the character's mask. What is the character's true motivation? Is the character to be trusted?

Choose a character and situation from the list below. Consider the events from the play so far and assume the character's persona as you complete the writing assignment.

- Write a letter from Hamlet to Ophelia explaining his actions so far.
- Write a letter from Gertrude to Claudius concerning Hamlet and the state of the country.
- Write a letter from Gertrude or Claudius to Rosencrantz and Guildenstern summoning them to Denmark.
- Write a letter from Horatio to either Gertrude or Ophelia regarding Hamlet's behavior.
- Write a letter from Polonius to Laertes regarding Ophelia or Hamlet.
- Propose your own persona letter.

Be sure you use language appropriate for your character. The content of the letter should reflect your interpretation of the character and the character's relationships and knowledge of the intrigues of the Danish court.

Response Questions

1. What assumptions about the character's personality and motives have you made?
2. What *segments* from the play or the character's lines helped you?
3. What *gaps* did you have to fill? How did you fill those gaps to flesh out your character?
4. What prior experience with characters, literature, drama, and life have you used to determine the validity of your interpretation of character?

Figure 4–5   Creating a Character: Persona Writing in *Hamlet*

© 2006 by Lisa Schade Eckert from *How Does It Mean?* Portsmouth, NH: Heinemann.

students from each respective class had different responses to the characters in the play. I never voiced my opinion about Ophelia's madness, but congratulated students on assuming, and arguing, an interpretive stance.

After we had read *Hamlet*, I asked students to write about the strengths and weaknesses of response theory as a final assessment of not only their work during the unit, but also to assess whether learning theory was making sense to them. Patrick's response was typical of the weaknesses some students perceived, which echoed the charges of relativism I described earlier in this chapter: "It's so abstract. No two people will ever have the same reaction. It's hard because there are no set rules."

Ashley wrote, "Each of us picks up on different things in the [work]. If we all thought the same way, it would be pretty boring and no one would learn very much or be open to new ideas." They learned to explore their initial "gut reaction," thinking about how that influenced their understanding of meaning. They also learned to question not only the text but their interaction with it, and the ways in which discussion can further clarify the ways they answer those questions. This is an important skill not only in understanding literary theory, but in processing many of the "texts" thrown at them by the world at large. Imagine having students question why a magazine advertisement or television commercial elicits an emotional response. Imagine if they question that response, or the criteria for validity they have unconsciously established to evaluate such advertisements positively or negatively.

Further Teaching Suggestions

- Ask students to think back to the reading strategies they learned in the early grades and consider how similar they are to the interpretive strategies (theory) they've been learning so far. See how many connections they can make.

- Model reader-response theory by following the steps in the Reader-Response Concept Map with a news article. How do readers' experiences (both in life and with journalistic writing) influence their understanding of the news? Compare coverage of the same story in different news sources to see if students feel they respond in the same way.

- Teach a difficult story, one that might have unfamiliar concepts or structure, and an easy one. Have students consider how they construct meaning using segments and filling in gaps. What makes a story "easy" or "hard"? What do readers do differently when the story is difficult?

More Readings for Teaching Response Theory

The Gorilla Signs Love by Barbara Brenner

A Separate Peace by John Knowles

A Wrinkle in Time by Madeleine L'Engle

5 Biographical Criticism: Teaching Voice and Theme

In ev'ry Work regard the Writer's End,
Since none can compass more than they intend.
                    —Sir Philip Sidney

Meaning requires a meaner.
                    —E. D. Hirsch, Jr.

In teaching genetic theory, I wanted students to see how consciously using personal information about the author and specific details about the time period depicted in a text would help them construct meaning from a text. I borrowed the term "genetic" from Donald Keesey's *Contexts for Criticism* (1987) to cover both biographical and historical approaches to reading literature, and to describe an approach that "seeks to reconstruct the original context of production (the circumstances and intentions of the author and the meanings a text might have had for its original readers) . . . [and] celebrate the text and its author as it seeks to make an original message accessible to readers today" (Culler 1975, 64). Students were familiar with biography as a genre and history as a subject, so it was easier to capitalize on their respective prior knowledge as a starting point. Without an understanding of these issues "the reader is without history, biography, psychology; he is simply that someone who holds together in a single field all the traces by which the written text is constituted" (Barthes 2001, 1469). I wanted to see just how much difference prior knowledge of the author and time period really made in student comprehension of text, partially because most of the anthologies students had used throughout their English studies emphasized such approaches. How much had the biographical and historical emphasis of their textbooks informed the ways they constructed meaning? I hoped they would recognize this approach as yet another method for reading and interpreting text.

Essentials of Biographical Criticism

Central to the biographical or authorial theory is, obviously, an understanding of the author of a given work. At its most basic, biographical criticism centers on the argument that it is not necessarily what the text says that is important, but because the author wrote with specific intentions in mind, the reader must reconstruct the author's intended meaning to reach the most accurate interpretation. While the text itself is an important source of clues for the author's outlook on life, the reader must go beyond the text to fully comprehend the author's use of language, major influences, and personal life events that may have contributed to the work. Understanding becomes "the construction of *another's* meaning . . . It is natural to speak not of what a text says, but of what the author means" (Hirsch 1987, 37, emphasis in original). When the reader can accurately assume the author's perspective, in a sense reenacting the author's stance throughout the text, then the reader can come closest to discovering the authorial voice and, consequently, the basic messages inherent in the work. Concrete facts about an author's life and language can be verified, helping to narrow the range of meaning possibilities and validating an interpretation as being the closest one to the author's intended meaning. It is the *author's* language, not the reader's, which defines the range of meaning possibilities.

Researching and responding to a significant individual's biographical history is a commonly used research project at all educational levels and content areas; I was certain that my students had been through such research before. Even though the anthologies used in the existing literature curriculum emphasized the personal history of authors, I did not know if students had fully explored how the details of an author's family, social, and psychological life offer a perspective for understanding that author's works. Too often the lesson ends with finding and recording facts about an artist's birth, death, and accomplishments, with no higher cognitive application for researched information. I decided that in World Literature, we would go beyond the basic research exercise and experiment with biographical criticism as a way to construct meaning from text. I did not, however, include specific references to the critics I have discussed in detail above, but rather adopted a general view of authorial biography as interpretive method.

Franz Kafka

Our most extensive exploration of biographical criticism centered on the life and works of Franz Kafka. This was due in part to the inclusion of Kafka's work in the textbook and World Literature curriculum, and in part because students often found his writing difficult to understand. I wanted to see how students would fare with Kafka's work if they assumed a biographical stance. Not only did students come to a better understanding of his work, but they sympathized with the man and his eccentricities, and gained an appreciation of the impact of reading any work with a biographical perspective. I encouraged them to draw conclusions from his works as interrelated pieces, not just individual stories, using each piece as a starting point for interpreting the next piece. Working with *The Metamorphosis*, *The Trial*, *The Castle*, and the movie *Kafka*, we investigated the concepts of voice and style, theme, and, of course, meaning. In addition, we reviewed the concepts of structural, response, and archetypal theory throughout the unit.

I assigned Part 1 of *The Metamorphosis*, giving no information on Franz Kafka, but asked students to examine how the story was constructed. I purposefully began with a structural emphasis so they could experience the difference in knowing and not knowing the author on their actual interpretive methods. Students noted the division of the story into three sections and pointed to the dramatic and, for them, unbelievable, first sentence. But a structural approach didn't help them construct a significant or unifying meaning for the rest of Part 1. "There's no way this could ever happen! This story is crazy," several students protested. "He's probably dreaming and will wake up any second and go 'Whew! What a dream!'"

It's true that the story requires an enormous leap of faith on the part of the reader, and this made it difficult for them to assume any stance toward the work at all. For some students, the whole concept was too large a leap and they resisted a serious study of the work, simply assuming that Gregor would wake up in the end. Our textbook translation read that Gregor Samsa discovers one morning he has turned into an enormous "dung beetle."

"What is a dung beetle, anyway?" Danielle wanted to know. Unfortunately, there was a picture of a large, black beetle in their textbook, which immediately formed their interpretation of Gregor's transformation. We parsed the word: dung is another word for feces, while of course a beetle is a bug with a protective shell. "Oh, a shit bug!" laughed Patrick, much to the amusement of the rest of the class. This wasn't helpful. We discussed this translation and compared it to other translations of the first sentence, in which Gregor has transformed into a "vermin" or "cockroach." Is turning into a "vermin" different from turning into a "dung beetle"? We talked about segments and gaps, and students tried to answer their questions about the information that they felt was missing from the narrative. They noted that the picture of the beetle that accompanied the first page of text filled in some gaps for them, but, because they were becoming increasingly critical of what they read (and saw, in this case), they weren't sure they could rely on it as an accurate interpretation.

They decided they disliked the father and began to sympathize somewhat with Gregor, but they didn't understand how Gregor transformed and what it could possibly mean. To help them develop a better understanding of Gregor and make a connection with Kafka himself later, when we would specifically address a biographical approach, I asked them to list reasons why they thought Gregor was unhappy even before he turned into a dung beetle. They noted his exhausting job, his father, money, responsibilities to his family, and his lack of friends, finding that they had more information about Gregor than they had thought. After the first section had thoroughly confused and intrigued them, they were primed for understanding the benefits of approaching a work biographically. Knowing about Franz Kafka himself, I hoped, would help them to construct meaning from the text.

First, to introduce them to Kafka more intimately than the sanitized, textbook paragraph of "author background," I gave students a few excerpts of Kafka's personal writing (see the excerpts at the end of this chapter). I had chosen these excerpts from Kafka's journals and "Letter to His Father" (Kafka 1974) to correspond with people and events in *The Metamorphosis*. Kafka was a prolific letter and journal writer, leaving an overwhelming body of primary sources, so I felt it was important to carefully choose appropriate excerpts. I didn't want to overwhelm students with the minutia of his personal writing or the wealth of secondary biographical sources that interpret that minutia.

As they read the journal excerpts, I asked students think about Kafka and his troubles in life, listing some of his problems and comparing them with the problems they listed for Gregor Samsa. They were amazed at the similarities between the two lists. "He's just like Gregor! I feel sorry for him." "Why didn't he just move out of the house? Couldn't he just leave?" "That's why the father in the story is such a jerk. Kafka's father was mean, too." "He probably really did feel like a bug!" Their curiosity was piqued; they wanted to know more about this man. They recognized elements of his voice in Gregor's words, or vice versa.

As with the previous perspectives in literary theory we studied, I started the unit with a study guide and discussion of the biographical approach (Figure 5–1). Students immediately grasped the concept, and had some thoughts about authorial theory as interpretive method.

"That's not for just writers, though," said Amy. "If you know anybody's personal history, you can understand why they do some of the things they do."

"Like politicians, or movie stars. Maybe Marilyn Manson was abused by his mother or something. That would explain him, sort of," mused Ryan.

"What about the (hypothetical) kid down the hall you think is weird?" I asked. "If you knew his personal background, could it change the way you understand him?"

Biographical Criticism

A biography is the story of a person's life. Biographies fulfill our human need to understand one another, explaining why and how an individual did certain things and helping us to understand the person's motivation and purpose. We can "walk in their shoes" for awhile, momentarily catching a glimpse of their perspective of the world and developing a certain amount of sympathy for their individual circumstances.

Knowing the biographical details of an author's life helps the reader to understand the author's *purpose* in writing a story, novel, or poem. Every author has a *message* to communicate; if the reader understands the author's purpose or motivation, then the reader can more clearly grasp that message. In fact, many biographical critics believe that the only way to fully understand the work itself is to understand the person who wrote it. The meaning readers understand, then, should be the author's intended meaning. It is also easier to understand an author's message if you have developed some sympathy for the author. Who is he or she? Why did he or she feel it was important to communicate to us? Have the author's life events contributed to the novel, story, or poem and the message communicated through the work?

How do you know what the author intended, even if the author lived a long time ago? Through research, finding out everything you can about an author's life, language, and personal beliefs and learning to recognize the author's *voice* speaking to you through the events and characters in a story. When you know about the author and can "hear" the author's voice, then the author's message to you is clearer, and you can find the meaning of a story, novel, or poem.

Thinking Biographically

Do you have a friend whom others may find difficult to get along with? How do you manage? Does knowing this person's personal reasons for acting the way he or she does help you? Explain.

Figure 5–1   Biographical Criticism
© 2006 by Lisa Schade Eckert from *How Does It Mean?* Portsmouth, NH: Heinemann.

"Yeah, sometimes other people don't like a couple of my friends. But I know them pretty well, and I know why they act the way they do. So it doesn't bother me," offered Patrick. "I guess that's like understanding the writer helps to understand the book."

"Do *all* writers have weird lives?" asked Tom, suddenly changing the subject.

"Well," I answered, "I guess you'd have to be a sensitive person to be a poet, or at least a person with the luxury of time on your hands to write seriously." (I think of Thomas Gray's "mute, inglorious Milton" lying in a country churchyard.) "Why do you think people want to become writers, or any kind of artist for that matter? Do all writers musicians, and artists make a lot of money?"

The class thought for a minute. "Not very many, really" said Kristi. "I don't think they really want to *become* artists, I think they just *have* to tell a story or play music." This class wasn't quite sure why an individual would choose these types of occupations. "Maybe your life has to have been difficult so you know about the problems other people might have, too."

"Does knowing the author change the way you understand a poem or story?"

"Lots of books have author notes on the back," said Danielle. "Sometimes I read those."

"Maybe you just don't really get the real point of anything you read," said Matt. "Maybe you just don't really understand it if you don't know about the author. But who cares, if you like the book anyway?"

"What if I just want to read without having to know everything about the author? What if I just like the story?" Jacob wanted to know.

I wondered if, when students began to understand an author's perspective, they would "hear" the author's voice and comprehend the author's message within a work. Could they develop sympathy for the author and an insight into the craft of creating setting and character as a vehicle for that message?

Voice and Theme

If the assumption is made that the voice in the text is the author's (which, in Kafka's works, I felt was a safe assumption), hearing the author's verbal meaning through the written words on the page requires some knowledge of the author's personality. Just as verbal conversation relies on the extraneous details of facial expression, tone of voice, and nonverbal gesture to communicate the meaning of words, so does this approach to constructing textual meaning rely on the extraneous details of the author's connotations for words, general outlook on life, and probable verbal intent in any communications. The basic elements of an author's voice and style remain fairly consistent throughout many of the author's works. When students can discern the author's voice in the text, they can see that author as a real human being with a story to tell and a message to convey. I hoped, by understanding how an author communicates ideas, students could find their own voices in writing and better communicate their own ideas or tell their own stories (Figure 5–2).

We went back to Kafka's personal journals and letters again to identify his voice and compare specific words and phrases with those of Gregor.

Voice in Writing
How Does the Author Speak to You?

When the phone rings and you pick it up, do you ever know immediately who is on the other end of the line? How can you tell? Is it the words the person says, the immediate subject of the conversation, or the tonal quality of the actual voice on the line? Often, it is not difficult to distinguish the voices of family and friends because you know them well, even if you weren't prepared to hear from them, by the characteristics of their speaking voices.

And every individual has not only a speaking voice, but also a writing voice. Sometimes we can tell who the writer is from the writing on a piece of paper because we recognize the writer's choice of words, subject matter, and the actual flow of the script. It's surprisingly easy to identify who wrote you a note if the person is someone you know well.

Everyone has distinctive characteristics about both their verbal and writing voice, and part of understanding an author's works is hearing the author's voice within the story, poem, or novel. Whenever we read a story, we have a sense of the individual who carefully chose words to create the characters, setting, and complications in a particular way to establish a particular position or opinion about the subject matter of the work. Then, just like a conductor in an orchestra, the author directs these inventions with some end result in mind. It is this sense of convincing authorial voice that controls the work and persuades the reader that it is a believable and worthy creation. In a sense, you "hear" the author throughout the story.

Identifying the author's voice is very much like identifying your friends' or family members' voices. If you become familiar with the author and with the author's works, you'll begin to recognize patterns in language, the subject matter, and elements of plot.

Thinking About Voice

Compare Kafka's personal writing from his journal entries and excerpts from his fiction. What elements of his personal voice are consistent with his voice in his fiction? Do Gregor, Joseph K., and K. say things that are similar to Kafka's reflections in his journals? List similar word choices and subject matter you notice.

Look at some of your own writing on homework papers, tests, essays, and notes or letters you may have written to your friends. Note any words or phrases you may use over and over, or subject matter that you discuss. What can you recognize about your own voice? Are there passages that even you don't understand or feel you want to explain? Does your writing voice change from paper to paper? Is it different from your speaking voice? Explain.

Figure 5–2   Voice in Writing: How Does the Author Speak to You?

© 2006 by Lisa Schade Eckert from *How Does It Mean?* Portsmouth, NH: Heinemann.

Kafka writes of the "uproar" and "inconsiderate" noise of his household as if it is unbearable. The most routine activities of a family's preparation for the day become magnified; the "slamming," "shouting," and "singing," and even the "hushing that claims to be friendly" of his father's leaving for work only lead to a "more distracted," "more hopeless noise" of the day to come. He contemplates finding the solitude for writing with words like "yearning" and "desire," bemoans the "agony" and "hedged in" feeling of working and, most important, refers to himself as a "snake" or "worm." Similarly, Gregor describes his job as "grueling" and "torture" and describes himself as "a tool of his boss, without brains or backbone." His father speaks to him in a "deeper, warning voice" and wears "a hostile expression" while he marvels at his mother's "soft voice." Gregor has transformed into a vermin, while Kafka only referred to himself as one. In his personal writing, Kafka's voice is clear and authentic ("straight up," according to Matt) because he wrote those words only for himself. In the stories, even though he has removed himself personally from the situation through his characters, students could clearly recognize his voice in both the narration and the voice of Gregor. Developing an ear for Kafka's voice helps students recognize the message inherent in the text, or, as a biographical critic might say, assume his stance or perspective as they interpret the events in his work.

Kafka, I must acknowledge here, is not the most appropriate author for studying the particulars of voice. We read his words in translation; his true voice is garbled somewhat by the translator of the text. But his life and work truly fascinated students as they discussed differences in various translations and particulars of his voice. As we studied his works, we discussed the understated power of the first sentence of each work, the melancholy nature of dialogue and description so characteristic of Kafka. These distinctly recognizable elements of voice allow students to readily hear him and grasp his message. To this end, and at this level of literary study, trusting in the translation gave students the opportunity to identify the voice telling the story as distinctly Kafka's.

Teaching theme as "the author's message to the reader" further connects the author and the text, giving students another angle from which to approach a work (Figure 5–3). Students could identify the author's voice, connect it to his life events, interpret and evaluate, then accept or reject his message by completing a log as they read (Figure 5–4). The theme or message of a literary work conveys what we identified at the beginning of this unit as the author's perception of an inherent truth about the world in which he lived. I discovered later that the greater concept of "perceived truth" served as a starting point for the larger student-inquiry projects I describe in Chapter 6, but in the beginning we simply discussed this as an aspect of theme.

Recognizing Theme

The Author's Message to You

The "theme" of a novel, short story, or poem is basically the message the author desires to communicate to the reader. Themes are communicated through plot design, setting, and character interaction. Once you have learned to recognize the author's voice, it is easier to hear the author's message and identify the major themes within a given work or in the author's body of work. The author had a purpose in mind and through writings communicates basic ideas about people, life, and living. Knowing about the author can make a theme within the works clearer.

For example, a theme traditionally associated with *Alice in Wonderland* is the contrast between the inherently illogical nature of the societies in which we live and our desire to logically organize our lives. Louis Carroll was a mathematician, and examines Alice's actions, her surroundings, and the characters she meets in a completely logical way, with some pretty strange (and very funny) results. If you were to read the novel again, understanding Carroll's mathematical background and intent to present the events in a purely logical way, you may be surprised at how much sense the seemingly senseless characters and situations actually make. The story can take on a completely different meaning.

Now that you have examined Franz Kafka's voice and understand his personal background and intentions, think about the message he communicates throughout his works. Examine the characters, actions, reactions, setting, and plot sequences from the perspective of a man like Kafka. Can you hear his message? How is he communicating to you? The events of any of his stories may seem absurd, but he presents them to the reader with purpose in mind. Can you understand his purpose more clearly as you hear his voice?

As you read and recognize elements of Kafka's voice and message within his works, record your examples and ideas on the Kafka Record Sheet. Spell out the relationship between each character, event, or specific plot sequence you note as important and any details you may have discovered about Kafka's personal life that explain the significance of that character or plot sequence. Finally, indicate the message you believe Kafka communicates through these aspects of the story. The message may be the same for several of your examples. Remember to record page numbers for each of your examples; the information here will help you write the essay at the end of the unit.

When you've taken some time to complete this chart with examples from several of Kafka's works, think about what you've learned.

Figure 5–3   Recognizing Theme: The Author's Message to You

© 2006 by Lisa Schade Eckert from *How Does It Mean?* Portsmouth, NH: Heinemann.

Kafka Record Sheet		
Character, Event, Quotation (Include source and pg #)	**Facts About Kafka** (Include source and pg #)	**Theme or Message Communicated**

Figure 5–4   Kafka Record Sheet

Initially, students had difficulty clearly expressing a theme. They wanted to use short, one- or two-word statements like "alienation" or "family relations" to describe the message they perceived. I encouraged them to express a theme in depth, using a complete sentence that was focused and specific. For example, rather than simply arguing for an author's sense of "alienation" as a theme, I pressed students to develop something closer to an exploration of "the problem of a person's alienation from society and the coping mechanisms needed for surviving as an individual." As we read from Kafka's work, the class brainstormed themes like these: "There are consequences for refusing to conform to an authority's opinion of who we are and what we should do"; or "Real communication between individuals is impossible, because we are all separate and have our own ideas about the world." It was interesting to discuss the relevance of theme to both the structuralism and biographical unit. When a reader assumes a structuralist stance, theme becomes a fundamental concept or issue that supports and enhances the plot, like the irony themes we had discussed during our reading of *Oedipus Rex*. But when a reader assumes a biographical or historical stance, theme becomes an issue relevant to the author's background and history, which, the reader can assume, the author desires to communicate through the story or poem. Realizing this difference emphasizes the importance of critical perspective. Once again, the discussion of and practice in identifying a specific theme also served as a foundation for the next unit.

Reading from *The Trial* and *The Castle* helped students continually review what they knew about the author and use that knowledge to construct meaning, emphasizing the relevance of a biographical approach. Both novels are fast reads, but I assigned only key chapters as required reading and allowed students to read the rest on their own to conserve time. Reading one of the novels entirely and a synopsis of the other could also help with the time crunch. The first chapters are obviously essential, and the last chapters of both novels end dramatically. Picking two or three key chapters from the novels to emphasize in class helped students to examine the same themes they identified in *The Metamorphosis*. I also found a great film, entitled *Kafka*, to use as the culmination of our Kafka unit. Starring Jeremy Irons as Franz Kafka, the movie cleverly blends bits from his personal history and writing in a plot of mystery and intrigue. The opening scene is extremely dramatic, drawing viewers immediately into the plot, and students delighted in recognizing subtle allusions to the works they had read. To top it off, the movie is a bizarre mystery (Kafkaesque, of course!) incorporating his major themes, including surrealistically slow chase scenes and strangely aloof characters—all of which helped students review the themes and the works they had studied as they watched.

By the time we had finished the movie, the class had completed a thorough review of Kafka's most important works, including the concept of voice and theme; they had even noticed similar structural patterns that emerged. The most striking linguistic pattern was the power of the first sentence in each work, as Kafka throws the reader right into the thick of the plot. Another pattern that emerged was Kafka's use of surrealistic elements. Students recognized that Kafka's voice and themes contribute to a mysterious and dreamlike quality in his work.

Authorial Biography and Media Literacy

Because students were already familiar with using encyclopedias and other basic sources for finding biographical information, and because grasping the concept of using authorial intent as an interpretive strategy wasn't a complex one for students, I could use this particular approach to teach in-depth research skills and encourage inquiry-based research projects without confusing them with too much information. Our school media center had recently added a new computer lab and updated electronic sources, which I was eager to introduce to students. I worked with the library media specialist to develop some guidelines for student research, using both in-depth print sources and electronic sources for gathering biographical information. Technology allowed the students greater flexibility in devising research topics and research questions, then locating and examining journals, letters, and personal artifacts from an author to help them gain perspective on the author's mind and message. For this unit we researched Franz Kafka, but the experience laid the foundation for the research that students would be doing in the final unit, described in the next chapter. The key was to make sure students used the author's background material as a springboard to interpretation, developing a feel for the author's point of view and intent in writing a particular piece. I used the concepts of theme and voice to encourage students to do so.

After reading excerpts of Kafka's personal writing and discussing themes from *The Metamorphosis*, *The Trial*, *The Castle*, and the movie *Kafka*, students had enough information to formulate a research question. Our goal was to see how much knowing about Kafka's personal history would help inform a final interpretation of his body of work. But I had struggled with deciding when students should write their research questions. Should it be before they read or after? Should it inform their immediate interpretation of the text, or round out a reading as they reflected on their knowledge of the author? I decided to have students do much of the reading first because I was looking to emphasize biographical criticism in stages of understanding; I wanted students to recognize the influence that prior knowledge of the author had on them so they could see if it made a difference in the way they interpreted the stories. Using the theme they had chosen as their basis of inquiry, students formulated research questions that directed their investigation into Kafka and his works. Their research questions evolved directly from their own curiosity, with a few guidelines from me. I required that each research question contain two or three basic concepts about Kafka, his message, and his works. For example, one aspect of Kafka's writing that we discussed was his use of surrealism and how he used its dreamlike images in his work (one student expressed this theme as "surviving a life you hate can be a nightmare"). The dreamlike state of Gregor's predicament in *The Metamorphosis,* the nightmare of Joseph K.'s experiences in *The Trial,* the strange way the Castle seems farther and farther away as K. tries to reach it in *The Castle,* and the agonizingly slow chase scenes in the movie *Kafka* are examples of surrealism that students readily identified. A pattern that remains consistent and is easily traced throughout Kafka's body of work, surrealism is an effective concept for a biographical, thematic focus. A research question engendered by a student's interest could be "Why did Kafka include surrealism so often in his works?" This deceptively simple question addresses (1) Kafka himself, (2) surrealism, and (3) any of his works. More complex questions like, "Does Kafka's need to be separate from his family and coworkers show up in a positive or negative way in his characters? Do they all have the same need to be alone or different, and does this turn out to be a good or bad thing?" includes Kafka, his theme of the innate separateness of the individual, and his main characters. Researching the answers to their own questions encouraged students to continue investigating Kafka's voice and theme, and to use the information they uncovered as a basis for understanding his work.

By articulating these questions, students progressed from a state of mystification at the first reading of *The Metamorphosis,* through a period of fairly self-directed inquiry, to a final determination of meaning and thematic understanding of the man and his message. Because they had followed their own research paths to answer questions they had posed themselves, they had something to say when they wrote reflective essays at the end of the unit. For example, Matt focused on how Kafka "shows how he believed in being alone as well as his dislike of society. Throughout his writing signs of despair and loneliness come into play continuously. In this novel [*The Castle*], the main character, K., never had a solid foundation to stand on. He was an outcast who apparently was satisfied with who he was and did not seem to care one bit about others around him. K. did not receive people well and had a hard time making friends."

He goes on to describe Gregor, who "represented Kafka himself associating every event that happened to Gregor with that of his own life. When Gregor became the beatle [*sic*], his family turned against him, especially his father as 'he went for Gregor with a sullen look on his face . . . and Gregor staggered at the . . . soles of his boots.' Reflecting on Kafka's life, this piece represents society attacking him. Kafka was the little ant on the street who always felt like he had to run for his life when people came walking by." Matt assumes Kafka's perspective on life, gained through reading his journal excerpts.

Danielle wrote, "Even though Kafka is now a renowned writer his life was not so magnificent. Kafka never accepted society, or himself for that matter. His works represent him as well as the people around him, exemplifying a different part of society and how it feels to be at the bottom of the social ladder."

Kristi realized that the "alienation felt by Franz Kafka led him into a life of isolation, an isolation then carried over to his stories, bringing to life characters much like himself."

Jacob compared Kafka's sense of isolation with Gregor Samsa's. "He was forced not only into mental isolation but also physical. 'It took great self-control for him [Gregor] to stay under the couch . . . in his cramped position where he could hardly breath' but he did it for his family so they wouldn't have to see him looking as he did. This forced isolation led Gregor into an unhappy, short life much the same as Kafka. Franz Kafka was a very isolated man and through his grotesque tales he showed his feelings by creating characters mirroring himself."

Bringing the themes and details of the author's life to light increases the likelihood of broad-based critical discussion in a classroom concerning feminist, ethnic, gay and lesbian, cultural, and post-colonial issues. That an author is from a marginalized population, is female, a minority, gay or lesbian, or oppressed by a dominant culture or social class becomes impossible to ignore. Such an author, almost by default, becomes representative of that culture, class, race, or gender; a teacher's decision to include a multicultural or marginalized literary work is a decision to include a voice that will speak for the author's segment of the population. Consequently, learning about a biographical and historical approach to constructing meaning was an important starting point for my students. As they began to inquire into the lives and times of the authors they chose to read during the remainder of the school year, new worlds opened up to them. This unit laid a crucial part of the foundation for the next unit, during which their inquiry drove our study of literature not only further into the postmodern landscape than I ever thought we'd go, but also into the darkest realms of human experience. And I didn't even plan it that way.

Further Teaching Suggestions

- Have students explore the controversy surrounding Forest Carter, the author of *The Education of Little Tree*, who was clearly not writing about his own life in the novel, even though it was touted as autobiographical. Does it change the meaning of the story to know that the author had invented his identity in writing the book?

- Review *Siddhartha* but include information about Herman Hesse. Is it more important to know about the society in which Hesse wrote, or the ancient Indian society depicted in the novel? How does it change the meaning for you to know about the author and his society?

- Compare the two excerpts of Kafka's journal from November 5, 1911, shown on the next page. Version 2 is from *The Decisive Years*, translated by Shelly Frisch (2005). Note the ways in which translations can differ but remain true to the author's voice.

More Readings for Teaching Voice and Theme

The Bomb by Theodore Taylor

Call of the Wild or *White Fang* by Jack London

Dragonwings by Lawrence Yep

Their Eyes Were Watching God by Zora Neale Hurston

A Tree Grows in Brooklyn by Betty Smith

Franz Kafka

His Personal Musings

November 5, 1911 (version 1): I want to write, with a constant trembling on my forehead. I sit in my room in the very headquarters of the uproar of the entire house. I hear all the doors close, because of their noise, only [the sound of] the footsteps of the people running between them are spared me. I hear even the slamming of the oven door in the kitchen. My father bursts through the doors of my room and passes through in his dragging dressing gown, the ashes are scraped out of the stove in the next room. Valli asks, shouting into the indefinite through the anteroom as though through a Paris street, whether Father's hat has been brushed yet, a hushing that claims to be friendly to me raises the shout of an answering voice. The house door is unlatched and screeches as though from a catarrhal throat then opens wider with the brief singing of a woman's voice and closes with a dull manly jerk that sounds most inconsiderate. My father is gone, now begins the more delicate, more distracted, more hopeless noise led by the voices of the two canaries. I had already thought of it before but with the canaries it comes back to me again, that I might open the door a narrow crack, crawl into the next room like a snake, and in that way, on the floor, beg my sisters and their governess for quiet (1974, 35).

November 5, 1911 (version 2): I sit in my room in the headquarters of the noise of the whole apartment. I hear all the doors slamming; their noise spares me only the steps of the people running between them; I can still hear the oven door banging shut in the kitchen. My father bursts through the door to my room and passes through, his robe trailing; the ashes are being scraped out of the stove in the next room; Valli asks, shouting one word after the other through the foyer, whether Father's hat has been cleaned yet; a hushing sound that aims to be friendly to me raises the screech of a voice in reply. The apartment door is unlatched and makes a grating noise like a scratchy throat, then opens wider with the singing of a woman's voice, and finally closes with a dull manly bang, which is the most inconsiderate sound of all. Father is gone; now the subtler, more diffuse, more hopeless noise begins, led by the voices of the two canaries. I had been thinking about it earlier, and with the canaries it now occurred to me again that I might open the door a tiny crack, slither into the next room like a snake and in that way, on the floor, ask my sisters and their governess for peace and quiet (21).

December 8, 1911: I have now, and have had since this afternoon, a great yearning to write all my anxiety entirely out of me, write it into the depths of the paper just as it comes out of the depths of me, or write it down in such a way that I could draw what I had written into me completely. This is no artistic yearning. (38)

December 28, 1911: The agony that the factory causes me. Why didn't I object when they made me promise to work there in the afternoons? No one used force to make me do it, but my father compels me by his reproaches. Karl [husband of Kafka's sister Elli] by his silence, and I by my guilty conscience. I know nothing about the factory, and this morning, when the committee made an inspection, I stood around uselessly with my tail between my legs. I deny that it is possible for me to fathom all the details of the operation of the factory. And if I should succeed in doing it by endlessly questioning and pestering all those concerned, what would I have achieved? I am fit only for cooking up something that looks all right, to which the sound common sense of my boss adds the salt that makes it look like a really good job. But through this empty effort spent on the factory I would, on the other hand, rob myself of the use of the few afternoon hours that belong to me, which would of necessity lead to the complete destruction of my existence, which, even apart from this, becomes more and more hedged in. (42)

From "Letter to His Father" 1919:
Dearest Father,
You asked me recently why I maintain that I am afraid of you. As usual, I was unable to think of any answer to your question, partly for the very reason that I am afraid of you, and partly because an explanation of the ground for this fear would mean going into far more details than I could even approximately keep in mind while talking. And if I now try to give you an answer in writing, it will still be very incomplete, because, even in writing, this fear and its consequences hamper me in relation to you and because the magnitude of the subject goes far beyond the scope of my memory and power of reasoning. . . .

You struck nearer home with your aversion to my writing and to everything that, unknown to you, was connected with it. Here I had, in fact, got some distance away from you by my own efforts, even if it was slightly reminiscent of the worm that, when a foot treads on its tail end, breaks loose with its front part and drags itself aside. To a certain extent I was in safety: there was a chance to breathe freely. The aversion you naturally and immediately took to my writing was, for once, welcome to me. . . . I was really quite glad of it, not only out of rebellious malice, not only out of delight at a new confirmation of my view of our relationship, but quite spontaneously, because to me that formula sounded something like: "Now you are free!" Of course it was a delusion . . . My writing was all about you; all I did there, after all, was to bemoan what I could not bemoan upon your breast. It was an intentionally long-drawn-out farewell from you, yet although it was enforced by you, it did take its course in the direction determined by me (Kafka 1974, 177–79).

Interpreting Character

What can you learn about this man by reading his journal entries? What makes him happy? What makes him sad? What problems does he have in life? Write a brief character sketch of him. Include your ideas about his physical appearance, his social life, his professional life. Cite examples from the excerpt or give reasons for your interpretation of his character.

6 Race, Class, Gender—and Philosophy: Teaching Students Thematic Criticism

Look beyond appearances and think about ways in which we would, with our own agency, intervene and transform the world.
> —Angela Davis

By the time we finished the biographical theory unit, the year was nearly two-thirds over. I was painfully aware that we still had many additional possibilities in the study of either literary theory or world literature. I mulled over a schedule for the weeks we had left in the school year, contemplating how we could cover as much theoretical and literary ground as possible. I had hoped to address certain aspects of modern theory: Marxism, feminism, postcolonial and cultural studies, maybe even deconstruction to shake things up a bit. How could I possibly introduce all these concepts and still cover a broad range of world literature? I would have to choose one or two ideas to teach and forget about the rest. I also wanted to provide time for students to choose a book and just *read*. I thought about my larger goals: to teach critical reading and interpretive strategies and encourage student engagement with text. Thus far students had readily grasped theory when I presented it in sequentially structured activities. What would happen if students also investigated theory on their own, settling on their own methods of interpretation? If I let students engage in their own inquiry, how could I be sure that they would have enough critical scaffolding to tackle difficult theoretical concepts and that the end of the year would not be a disaster? In the end, I decided once more to give my students the benefit of the doubt and trust that they could extend what they'd learned already and branch off on their own. The unifying framework would again be theory. I thought it would be interesting for students to try their hand at specific theoretical approaches—such as feminism, historicism, Marxism, deconstruction, and so forth, as separate and identifiable schools of thought—as they became increasingly self-directed. I condensed this into two general themes, sociological and philosophical, and introduced the basic concepts of each. "Thematic criticism" is a good umbrella term for this approach, providing a larger framework for many postmodern and traditional approaches to literary interpretation, but familiar enough for students to grasp the concept. Defined by Stanley Fish, thematic criticism explores "the literary expression of [various] concerns, be they economic, psychological, political or military, sexual. . . . what the thematic critic then produces are economic or psychological or sociological or political or philosophical readings" (1999, 106). In the course of this unit, students took the helm and I was often just along for the ride, so we did not advance in as neatly linear a fashion. I didn't provide study guides or questions, nor did I provide specific "background" information; instead, I decided to provide the larger frameworks of modern theory, but allow student-generated inquiry to tease out the finer points and further our study of literature and theory. Consequently, at times we discussed theory and terminology in tangential minilessons, tackling some larger concepts as they arose in full-class and small-group discussions.

I chose to focus on sociological and philosophical theory as themes because both invite further study of modern and historical thought, allowing students to focus their ideas without overly limiting their interpretative approach to any text they chose to read. I simply found I could not separate larger concepts of sociological theory from ideology. Sociological criticism implies more than the study of society; it includes the study of ideologies that privilege certain aspects of society while oppressing others, perpetuating the concept of the "other" in social stratification. Philosophical criticism, on the other hand, refers to a history of ideas but includes interpretive discussion of how these ideas are exemplified in a story, novel, or poem. Both themes allowed students the freedom to pursue historical and modern modes of inquiry and provided students with concrete guidelines and language for expressing their interpretation of literary material.

Sociological Criticism

It made sense to begin this larger scope of theory and interpretation with a sociological approach because it provided a logical progression from biographical criticism. M. H. Abrams defines such an approach as an "interest in the ways authors are affected by such circumstances of their time and place as their class status, gender, and interests, the ways of thinking and feeling characteristic of their era, the economic conditions of the writer's profession and of the publication and distribution of books, and the social class conceptions, and values of the audience to which writers address themselves. Sociological critics treat a work of literature as inescapably conditioned . . . by the social, political, and economic organization and forces of its age" (1988, 174). A sociological approach, therefore, offers the opportunity to explore ideological theories of race, Marxism, feminism, and cultural studies, while also opening the door for students to examine broadly historical approaches to constructing meaning from text. Because these are all-important issues in and of themselves, I will address them individually throughout my discussion of student activities and response.

Sociological theory is a stance toward a text in which the reader assumes that to really understand a literary work implies knowing something about either the society in which it was written or the one it depicts. Students grasped this concept quickly, and without any study guide, because they had some prior knowledge; they had been studying cultural and social history for years in school. To model this approach, I again revisited Gabriela Mistral's short story "Why Reeds Are Hollow," but this time I included the brief introduction, which gives a short biography of the author and additional information about the time and place in which it was written. I asked students to read the story once more, but this time to also consider how knowing about the author and the time period influenced their reading. Bill's response illustrated not only that he readily understood what it meant to use the history as a basis for understanding, but that he carefully paid attention to detail, using everything he knew to construct meaning: the only notation of the date of its publication is in the tiny copyright acknowledgment at the bottom of the last page:

> When this story was written, in 1914, World War I had started. In Europe, Germany was trying to grow bigger, change its shape, size and purpose. The story shows that everything has its natural shape, size and purpose and that it's wrong to try and change that. Everything should work together with their [*sic*] differences and there will be harmony . . . Knowing it was written during World War I makes this more meaningful.

I was pretty impressed that he noted the date of publication and used that information to further construct meaning from the story. Since students had read the story several times over already, they could focus on how to assume a broader, sociological stance rather than just the details of the story. Eli summed it up nicely, saying, "You just fill in the gaps with history." Amy wrote that she liked sociological criticism "because you can draw parallels between things in the society and have a better understanding of the work." They had to decide how they could use historical knowledge to fill in textual gaps, answer questions, and solve problems in the text, thereby supporting their interpretation of characters and events. It didn't take long to move on to more complex issues.

Ideology: Marxist and Feminist Theory

A discussion of sociology's role in literary interpretation inevitably involves addressing the subject of ideology. Ideology is "a set of concepts, beliefs, values and ways of thinking and feeling through which human beings perceive, and by which they explain, what they take to be reality" (Abrams 1988, 219). Ideology informs perception, but does not uncover, and can even obscure, an objective view of society and the world at large. All societies in history have perpetuated an ideology inherent in a system of values, beliefs, ideas, and customs with certain expectations for the behavior of the individual. Ideological assumptions help each of us determine how we fit in the world, what we believe, and how we should treat others, and are often unconscious, unarticulated, and embedded in daily social and personal interaction. We unconsciously hold to ideological paradigms that we've learned through the living of life and through contact with our social environment. An entire society can hold to a system of ideological beliefs, or it can be a private and individual belief system. Ideologies determine what is acceptable and what is not in a given society, and can lead to oppression of those in society who do not hold with the ideological beliefs of the majority. Raymond Williams defines ideology as a "set of ideas which arise from a given set of material interests or definite class or group" in society (1977, 156). Ideology is a political construct, actively causing an individual to behave one way or another in society even if the person is not aware of holding to the tenets of a specific ideology, and is often an emotional response to social and personal issues. It is, therefore, a cause rather than an effect, which, combined with the emphasis on material interests, draws a clear distinction from philosophy. Sociological criticism, then, examines the societal, or cultural, ideology within a text.

This was difficult stuff, and required students to keep an open mind and the willingness to "stretch." I hoped that by studying the concept of ideology first, students would be able to comprehend philosophical theory later. I began by asking students to analyze their own worldview, using a worksheet I called Ideology and You (Figure 6–1) to help them recognize the many people, events, and institutions that may have influenced them.

This met with varying degrees of success; while students could easily point to *someone else's* ideology, they had much more difficulty recognizing their own. When Ashley shared her ideological notion that people should treat others as they would like to be treated, Kristi objected, "That's not ideology! That's just doing what's right." Danielle intervened

---

Ideology and You

Ideology is the system of social, cultural, and personal values and beliefs that help you make sense of the world around you—your concept of right and wrong—and define expectations for behavior (yours and those around you). To explore your ideology, consider the following questions:

1. What or who has helped you determine who you are now, who you think you should be, and who you want to be in the future? Think about home, school, society, and/or religious affiliations.
2. How/where do you spend much of your time?
3. Can you think of any traditions (family or social) that may have shaped certain attitudes for you?
4. Do you have personality traits or behaviors that have been encouraged or discouraged? What are they and how are they encouraged or discouraged?
5. What are you most rewarded for in school? Why?

Reflect on the experiences you've had that may have shaped your ideology. See if you can state your ideological worldview in a couple of sentences.

Figure 6–1   Ideology and You

© 2006 by Lisa Schade Eckert from *How Does It Mean?* Portsmouth, NH: Heinemann.

with "That's what you think is right. Someone else might think that you should treat people any way you want to." I offered them this statement attributed to Karl Marx: "Man is the product of his environment, and of conditions; he cannot therefore be free in the choice of his profession, he cannot be the maker of his own happiness" (Riazanov 1996). Having been taught that they can be anything they choose to be (which is in itself an example of ideology), students overwhelmingly disagreed. "You can go to school, you can decide to be a lawyer or a doctor and go for it," said Ryan. "If you can't afford college, you can just get a scholarship or a student loan."

"If you work hard enough, you can do anything," argued Matt. Other students cited a number of individuals who validated this belief: Oprah Winfrey, Michael Jordan, Dave Thomas (the founder of Wendy's fast-food restaurants), Derek Jeter (our hometown hero), and several others. I asked them if they thought these individuals would have been successful in a different time or place; what if they lived in the Middle

East or China? "Well," said Danielle, "I guess no one in the Middle East cares about Oprah's low-fat diet." Matt said he felt fortunate for "the luck of being born here where anyone can get rich." I was struck that getting rich was the yardstick to measure a society's level of enlightenment.

"If that's true, then why isn't everyone rich?" I asked. "Who is it that gets rich in our society?" I wanted students to think about what factors determine whether an individual remains in an upper or lower class in our society. These students had grown up in what some might consider an enlightened age, yet most of them were surprisingly oblivious to oppressive forces that existed in their own culture or community. They were optimistic about what the future had in store for them, and how much they could control it, but had little concept of the existing societal system that made it easier for some individuals than for others to achieve economic and personal success.

To avoid overly confusing students and overtly influencing them with my own ideologies (although I acknowledge that it's impossible to teach from a completely neutral ideological stance), I furthered the concept of ideological theory as an interpretive stance and academic concept by introducing Marxism and feminism, rather than my own ideological beliefs, as vehicles for discussion. Both theoretical approaches to literature are particularly appropriate for exploring ideology, because they specifically and purposefully demonstrate the power of ideology and seek to make ideology visible (critical theorists call this "ideology critique"). In addition, issues we discussed in the context of Marxist and feminist theory also provided a framework for postmodern theories that some students would investigate later, such as cultural studies, postcolonial, gender, and minority theories of interpretation.

Marxist Theory

Karl Marx argued that, because we are all a product of social development, an individual's ideology is both consciously and unconsciously the result of societal class struggle. Because these students lived in an insulated suburban community, even though they may have come from an economically disadvantaged background, they were part of a privileged class and had difficulty recognizing how that had influenced their personal ideologies. Marxist theory allowed the students to draw upon previously studied theoretical approaches to literature as well as on their responses to the concept of ideology because it "typically undertakes to 'explain' the literature in any era by revealing the economic, class, and ideological determinants of the way the author writes, and to examine the relation of the resulting literary product to the social reality of that time and place" (Abrams 1988, 219). In this way, Marxist theory challenges the reader to recognize the inadequacies and injustices of a given social system—the hidden ideological agendas that result in the oppression of certain populations in society. The oppressed within a society often are unable to contribute to the literary output of the age; they are considered the "other" and their voices are not heard. This ideological struggle between the dominant and oppressed classes is the key to Marxist theory.

But Marxist theory also recognizes as great writers those who can transcend political boundaries and depict a more objective view of society, even if they do belong to the privileged class. For example, Charles Dickens enjoyed a fine London lifestyle, but accurately wrote of the injustices imposed on those characters who inhabited the seamy underbelly of London's prisons and alleyways (even though he did end many of his novels with a rich guy who saves the day). William Shakespeare's genius lies partially in his characterization of individuals hailing from all social classes, including his complex female characters. In the modern age, writers like Bertolt Brecht incorporated Marxist principles into their work. Brecht argued that literature should jar readers out of an acceptance of privileged priorities by challenging them to see society in a new light, stirring a desire for necessary change. This "estrangement effect" is part of the modernist experimentation with disruptive forms of drama and literature emphasizing the incoherencies of societal structure. Luigi Pirandello, Eugene O'Neill, and Jean Anouilh wrote dramas in the form known as "theatre of the absurd" to shock the viewer (or reader) into a closer scrutiny of society's ideologies.

Teaching Ideology Critique and Marxist Theory

First, I asked students if they had ever heard of Karl Marx. They had. Then I asked them if they knew when he lived, what he did, or who he was. They didn't, although one student asked, "Isn't his body stuck in a glass case somewhere in Russia?"

"No, that's Lenin," I answered, suppressing a smile. "Marx was his contemporary, though, and believed that the dominant classes or institutions in society perpetuate certain ideologies to keep society in order. It's about economics; whoever has money has power. Maybe your ideology tells you that anyone can be anything, like you said earlier, and that if you work hard enough you can be rich. But maybe that's what our society wants you to believe, so when people are not successful they will think it's their own fault. That's the *status quo*; keeping things the same, keeping society organized, keeping those who *have* power *in* power and making people think things are the way they should be in society so no one wants to change them."

"That's like school," someone muttered. "When we get in trouble it's always our fault, not like there's anything wrong with the rules."

"Well, yes, I suppose you could make that argument. Does anyone ever subvert the rules? You know, maybe break a tiny one just to show that it might be an unnecessary rule?" I was cautious, not wanting to perpetuate a subversive ideology and incite a revolution right there and then, but hoping to take advantage of the moment to make a point about Marxist theory as a means to construct meaning from text.

"Yeah!" Tom laughed. "I ate a candy bar right in front of the office this morning." (The principal had recently declared a moratorium on food in the hallways.) This started a small outcry about the injustice of starving students all day, since lunch period was very short and crowded. "So to subvert that rule gave you a sense of power or control, right? But you didn't really make a strong statement, like starting a resistance movement by selling candy bars to everyone in the hall. Sometimes that's what stories can do, just offer up a different ideology than those accepted by society (at least on the surface) to help people realize that there might be different ways of thinking about life. How can a story or an author support or subvert the status quo?" They thought for a minute and I was a little relieved when, instead of focusing on the school rules issue, Patrick changed the subject. "You can tell by who's the bad guy and who's the good guy, like in a movie. Like, if they think society is fine the way it is, then the bad guy is a robber or a criminal. If the bad guy is a cop or politician or something, then the movie is about problems in our society, right? Then we think about the problems like that, maybe get mad, and want to change them."

"Yes" I answered, pretty impressed with his insight. "Some Marxist theorists argue that literature often promotes the lifestyle of the privileged class in society. They pay attention to the biases of writing that impose privileged voices and ideologies, suspecting that the real message of most 'great' literature supports and legitimizes the status quo. They like writing that depicts the reality of all classes in society and lets somebody else talk for a while. Marxist critics value literature that is revolutionary and subversive, like stories and poems that try to expose the agenda, or ideology, of the privileged in order to change society. Eating that candy bar in front of the office on purpose was subversive. If you wrote a story about it, you'd be sharing a subversive message."

"Like Bart Simpson!" Kristi interrupted. "He's always getting in trouble at school, but he's pretty smart about the ways he does it. Every time I watch that show, I think about how dumb some of the rules are."

I laughed, because I love *The Simpsons* and had used excerpts from the show to illustrate satire; now I was thinking it would be a great way to illustrate ideology critique, even philosophy. "You're right! And the mayor doesn't come out any better than Principal Skinner." I moved on, wishing I had thought of using an episode today. "Think about *Siddhartha* again. Siddhartha had the choice to refuse his wealth and position in society; he could choose to search for the path to enlightenment. But what if he was poor and had to keep his family from starving? What if his father couldn't take care of everything for him after he left? What if he was from the untouchable class in India's caste society then? A Marxist critic would read the story differently, because Siddhartha isn't quite so admirable when all that is taken into consideration. The point is that there is always an economic consideration in a story, the question of who has power and who doesn't."

Since Marxist theory often centers on the political and revolutionary, I thought it would be best to practice by reading something that obviously exuded politics and class struggle. I modeled a Marxist reading of the prose poem "Journey Along the Oka" (Albert, et al. 1993, 1267–68), by Alexandr Solzhenitsyn. Solzhenitsyn, who was imprisoned as a leading literary critic of communism as practiced in the Soviet Union, uses church buildings as a central metaphor in the poem. The churches he describes house community activities but not religious worship, emphasizing the loss of not only religious freedom, but freedom in general under the Communist regime. In the final line, the status quo prevails over the quiet musings and stark descriptions of vandalized churches as the speaker is called to join in the community activities taking place on sacred ground. Even though it seems as though the speaker's participation is supportive of the status quo, the underlying ironic tone running throughout the poem illuminates its revolutionary theme. I read the poem twice, once to establish the metaphor of church buildings, then again to recognize the irony of the speaker's words. Then I directed students to read Mistral's "Why Reeds Are Hollow" yet one more time (they were finally becoming weary of it) and respond to the different details they noticed now that they knew a little something about Marxist theory. Kristi wrote that she now recognized it as "a story in which the higher class is wanting power and so the lower class suffers as a result of their greed. So a major 'social revolution' takes place among the plants."

We spent a few days reading *Kaffir Boy*, the autobiographical story of Mark Mathabane's childhood in Soweto, South Africa, during the years of apartheid. We didn't linger on the novel and students read it almost entirely on their own. I include it here because issues of race, oppression, and white privilege came up in their written responses. While most class members were still remarkably oblivious to their social position of privilege as that of middle- to upper-class white society, they were quite sympathetic to both the historical and contemporary oppression of minorities for racial affiliation and religious beliefs. For example, Melanie found that Mathabane "uses whites and their ideology to show how wrong they were. Schools were even teaching their students to look down on black people. Clyde's [a young, wealthy white character] mind is full of wrong information." Susan commented on the marginalization of black South Africans:

> This is what the black South Africans do; they make the money by working *for* the whites. Clyde says "That's why you can't live or go to school with us, but can only be our servants." This deals with the suppression of one class by another that will benefit by their power. Dr. Verward suppressed Africans, saying "Bantu education should not be used to create imitation whites." This is so that whites can remain established as the superior class.

Tom agreed that "in *Kaffir Boy*, the author is struggling against a society which he cannot change. The system protects itself. Apartheid never allowed the blacks to voice anything. They were forced into submission." Students were obviously getting the point.

The concepts of oppression and "other" also laid the foundation for a transition into feminist theory. While Marxist theory identifies societal struggle along the fault lines of upper and lower socioeconomic classes, feminist theory finds the struggle apparent in the patriarchal societal system that privileges men and subordinates women. Where Marxist theory recognizes class struggle in which the lower classes are oppressed, feminist theory recognizes a gender-based power struggle in which women are oppressed. The results are the same for the respective subordinated groups; the oppressed "other" in society is dispossessed of a voice. Both theoretical approaches to literature focus on representations of the tensions and contradictions that result from these societal stratifications. I was impressed with the students' response to societal marginalization, even though I was surprised by how little these World Literature students recognized the class-based power structure in their own society. But this did not prepare me for their initial response to feminist theory.

Feminist Theory

Feminist theory examines the presence and absence of women in literature, rejecting stereotypical characterization and interpretation of the male as the dominant, active, and rational being and the woman as the passive, submissive, and emotional being. Referring to women as an oppressed societal class, particularly in the realm of literature, is, without a doubt, historically and socially accurate. But more than just emphasizing this oppression, feminist literary criticism is "at once critical and enabling . . . [taking] issue with the way the male-dominated canon has represented women, and [finding] in the literary evidence signs of a counter-narrative, an alternative story of women's experience" (Ryan 1999, 104). In addition to examining female characters, feminist critics trace the development of female writers who had few role models and a limited literary tradition upon which to draw, establishing a counter-canon of women writers to recognize the contributions women have made in literary history.

I introduced feminist theory by revisiting Karl Marx's statement on an individual's freedom to find happiness in society. I did not tell students that they were now going to learn about feminist literary theory, I merely asked them who was missing from Marx's quote "Man is the product of his environment . . ." They were silent, absolutely puzzled by my question. "Look at the pronouns," I hinted. Nothing. "Who is he referring to?" Susan ventured a guess. "People, like, the people who don't have power?"

"Human beings, you know, mankind," Tom answered. "That's a dumb question."

"But which human beings?" I prodded. I waited a bit longer, until I was sure they weren't going to answer. "Why does he only refer to male human beings?" I finally asked. Groans erupted around the class.

"It's just a figure of speech!" Ryan said emphatically, throwing his arms in the air.

"But what are the implications of this 'figure of speech'?" I asked.

Jacob groaned, "Don't tell me you're one of those femi-nazis!"

"Yeah," Matt chimed in. "When will we talk about masculine criticism?"

I was stunned. I found myself hesitating, becoming almost apologetic as I answered, "You don't have to be militant to be a feminist critic; it's not an argument about man against woman, it's just another way to approach a text." None of the methods we had studied so far had elicited such a response, or the resistance that would follow, not even when I referred to the biblical stories of creation as myths, as I described in Chapter 2. In desperation, I looked at the young women in the class for support or some kind of reaction but they were, for once, unresponsive. What was going on? Class ended on that note, but I was thankful I would have some time to recover from this response, and better prepare myself for a discussion.

I felt responsible, to a certain extent, for these students' reactions to feminist theory because up to this point I had essentially adhered to the canonical "givens" in my curriculum, the textbook, and even in the theoretical approaches I had presented to students. And, because I was consciously trying *not* to reveal any bias I felt for either a theoretical approach or a particular text, I had not been openly challenging the "androcentric literary canon, [in which] men are able to see themselves (or possibilities of themselves), while women are forced to become the Other—to adopt a male persona, to see themselves as male, and to participate in an experience that can never be theirs" (Obbink 1992, 39). I felt strongly about the marginalization of women in the same way I felt strongly about the marginalization of minority populations who are forced into the role of "other." I wanted to know why this approach seemed to be so different for students than the other ideological theories. Feminist critic Dale Spendler (1982) points out that there is an underlying threat inherent in feminist theory: "Fundamental to the patriarch is the invisibility of women, the unreal nature of women's experience, the absence of women as a force to be reckoned with. When women become visible, when they assert the validity of that experience and refuse to be intimidated, patriarchal values are under threat . . . And when we assert that the reason for women's absence is not women, but men, that it is not that women have not contributed, but that men have 'doctored the records,' reality undergoes a remarkable change" (11). I believe it was this sense of "threat" that, in part, explains their reaction to feminist theory. I wanted them to understand that assuming a feminist perspective did not negate the importance of what they already knew about literature. Instead, it should *enhance* what they already knew, giving them one more way in to a text. So, when I brought the poem "Myth," by Muriel Rukeyser (Levi 1995, 252), to class the next day, I was hoping to encourage further discussion of feminist theory as an ideology, similar to Marxism and sociological criticism. I'm including the full text of the poem here, because it began a reenvisioning of the literature we had read so far and influenced student inquiry later that year.

Myth

Muriel Rukeyser

Long afterward, Oedipus, old and blinded, walked the
roads.   He smelled a familiar smell.   It was
the Sphinx.   Oedipus said, "I want to ask one question.
Why didn't I recognize my mother?"   "You gave the
wrong answer," said the Sphinx.   "But that was what
made everything possible," said Oedipus.   "No," she said.
"When I asked, What walks on four legs in the morning,
two at noon and three in the evening, you answered,
Man.   You didn't say anything about woman."
"When you say Man," said Oedipus, "you include women
too. Everyone knows that."   She said, "That's what
you think."

We read the poem together in class, and I asked students why it was that Oedipus didn't recognize his mother, according to the poem. After a period of silence, Danielle spoke up. "Because he only recognized men. If he had recognized the importance of women in his society, maybe he would have taken a closer look at Jocasta. I never could understand why he couldn't figure out who she was." True, Oedipus never gave evidence that he valued the ideas or significance of women in his society. How could he recognize Jocasta as his mother if he didn't recognize her as anything but a status and sex symbol? The play continually emphasizes the marriage bed, but what about the role of the queen in society and government? How could he truly "see" his situation if he was blind to the power of women in his life and society?

"That's like Gertrude, too," offered Kristi. "Maybe she married her brother-in-law because she didn't want to go live in a little house somewhere."

"Even if she didn't know Claudius murdered his brother, she still married him pretty fast. I think she was just looking out for herself—and Hamlet, too. I can't believe she was having an affair with him all along. Why would she risk that? Hey, maybe she was trying to protect Hamlet for real. Maybe she was afraid Claudius would kill him, too!"

"They were smart about their marriages anyway. They couldn't be king after their husbands were dead. They did the next best thing. What else could they do?"

"I think both of them knew a lot more than they let anyone else know. Why would Jocasta kill herself all of a sudden? Why did she want Oedipus to stop asking questions early on? She just blew him off and didn't want to think about it."

These students were right about the position of Jocasta and Gertrude as enigmatic central figures in *Oedipus Rex* and *Hamlet*. They both sustain a central core of action and theme development in the plays, but establishing their motivation isn't easy. How much do they know about the circumstances of their second marriages and when do they know it? Students reflected further on the social position of women in each play's society, the possibility that each character knows much more than she lets on, and that each woman married to retain her social position. Jocasta and Gertrude (Ophelia as well) each define their social and individual selves through a liaison with a man. These women struggle within the constraints and powerlessness of their femininity and position in society, trying to create or maintain a certain quality of life, and are undone.

Discussing the poem "Myth" had sparked students to question more carefully the role of women in some of what they had read. Laura Apol Obbink, in "Feminist Theory in the Classroom" (1992), points out the importance of such reflection and questioning in applying feminist theory: "Reentering texts is much more than an exercise in reading technique, for the silencing of women is part of a larger oppression . . . by asking different questions of the text—hearing different questions in the text—we can begin to value women's writings, and we can allow our students to do the same" (40).

"You know, I just thought of something," Eli mused. "Kamala is really the only person who had power, at least kind of, over Siddhartha. Even his father couldn't distract him like she did. But does that make her good or bad?" I reminded students that, even though we had studied primarily male heroes in the archetypal unit, the animus was also an important element of the female consciousness; women weren't just characters in literature to provide the anima, or romantic counterpart, to male heroes. Women, I argued, have been just as marginalized as the black Africans in the apartheid that had outraged them so much in *Kaffir Boy*. Many students were still dubious, arguing that women were considered equal to men these days. When I asked them why the Equal Rights Amendment never passed, they said it was because it wasn't necessary. When I asked them why women on average made less than men in the same jobs, they pointed to teachers' salaries, which are determined by a contractual scale and are the same for men and women. I was about to forget my vow to remain unbiased and launch into a comparison of the football and volleyball coaches' salaries, but I stopped, reminding myself that my ultimate goal was to teach theory and maybe it would be better to allow students to explore the idea in literature rather than reducing it to a localized classroom argument. Ashley broke the stalemate by suddenly volunteering her thoughts on *Emma*, by Jane Austen. "In that book, women had to find a man to have a life. All the girls did in the story was worry about who they were going to marry. But I don't think the author thought it was a bad thing, I think she liked it that way. So she was supporting the status quo of women only being wives and mothers, right?"

Obviously, I didn't resolve the issue of feminist theory, either pedagogically or ideologically, and wish I could report more favorably about my efforts in this class. But I'm telling my story, and this is the way it happened. Did I learn something? Absolutely. I learned that I needed to challenge the ways students gain prior knowledge (or what they think is prior knowledge) of feminism before addressing what feminist theory means as a way in to a text. I learned that we have so much further to go in admitting women into the mainstream literary canon; the way we *talk* about women in and as authors of literature is just as important as including works written by women. I learned that the media images of women continue to be dangerously powerful and insidious. This is an area that requires more study and attention, both in the scholarly application of and daily practice in teaching feminist approaches to constructing meaning from text.

Philosophical Criticism

As our final foray into the realm of theory, philosophical theory gave students some room for individual research and exposure to some of the important historical ideas about life and the living of it. As with archetypal theory, I didn't go into a lot of detail at first, but drew a clear distinction between ideology and philosophy. I will go into further detail here, before I describe the methods I used in the classroom, not to pedantically mince terms, but to explain my rationale for using these terms in the way I did with students. I wanted to open as many doors for student inquiry as possible while still providing frameworks for theoretically approaching literature.

Philosophy is "an academic discipline . . . whose traditions are special" according to Fish, and is "that area of inquiry in which one asks questions about the nature of truth, fact, meaning, mind, action and so forth, and gives answers within a predictable range of positions" (1999, 104). Philosophy is not arbitrary or individual but can be understood as a *product* of ideological, social, and psychological awareness: the examined life. Philosophers must examine the assumptions of their individual ideologies, societal ideologies, and historical ideologies in order to formulate a theory of philosophy. While ideology refers to sociopolitical theory, philosophy is a much broader topic; while ideology is active and causal, philosophy is academic and theoretical. Philosophy only becomes ideology when it is imposed on someone else. For example, a religious belief can be a philosophy, but becomes ideology when it is wielded in a social or political situation as a means of establishing power. An ideological belief can be developed into a school of philosophy when its basic premises are closely examined and objectified in the larger context of the philosophic tradition.

Everyone acts according to the tenets of an ideology, but philosophy can only be the result of closely examining the larger questions of life in general. Consequently, while the subject of philosophy is broader in aspect, there are fewer people engaged in philosophical contemplation than those engaged in ideological debate. Fish also argues that even though "the relevance of philosophy to every aspect of human culture has been assumed for so long that it now seems less an assertion or an argument than a piece of plain common sense," this understanding of philosophy is erroneous because it is based on the "debatable proposition that almost everything we do is a disguised and probably confused version of philosophy" (1999, 104). Philosophy is the larger process of consciously and rationally developing a conclusion about life and the purpose of living, not merely a rationale explaining why people do the things they do. Raymond Williams (1977) distinguishes between ideology and philosophy by noting that "sensible people . . . have a *philosophy*; silly people rely on *ideology*" (157, emphasis added). Assuming a philosophical stance in approaching text first requires an understanding of the particular philosophical thought itself, much like assuming an archetypal stance means understanding the concepts of archetypes and the representation of the Jungian self. So philosophical interpretation can be understood as the recognition of this structure in the text, making it a more objective approach than when the reader assumes an ideological stance.

Philosophical criticism, then, can be defined as a method of constructing interpretation by applying philosophical schools of thought (e.g., existentialism, creationism), the theories of an historic philosopher (e.g., Hume, Kierkegaard, Nietzsche), or even a specific theology (e.g., Buddhism, Christianity, Hinduism) as prior knowledge for unlocking the text. In other words, the reader, in this case, uses the basic tenets of a philosophical theory to fill in the gaps and link segments of a text, very much like the interpretive process students used for the archetypal approach. Although Fish argues that philosophy and literary theory are distinctly different subjects of study, he acknowledges that "traditions of philosophy and literary criticism display certain points of intersection . . . in the past twenty-five years philosophy has become something that literary critics do or attempt to do" (1999, 104). A specific philosophy can be applied to a work regardless of the work's form, author, or place in history. For example, an existentialist approach is not limited to works by existentialist philosophers such as Jean-Paul Sartre or Albert Camus. In fact, recent trends in young adult fiction lean toward stark realism and provide excellent vehicles for existential discussion. Because, as Fish pointed out, the term *philosophy* has often been used loosely to encompass various ideological views, I wasn't surprised when students initially asserted that each individual has a personal philosophy and life. When I asked them what their philosophy was, I received a barrage of answers. "I think you should just have fun every day," said Matt. "Do unto others as you would have them do to you," offered Amy. "Seize the day!" said Jacob.

"Well, those are really either your personal ideologies or proverbial sayings, but not exactly philosophy," I pointed out.

"Humph! It's my philosophy, anyway" Jacob muttered.

"Let's think about how philosophy is different from ideology," I said. I gave students the handout Philosophy and All of Us (Figure 6–2), offering some guidelines about distinguishing between the two concepts.

We read this together, and I cited Socrates as the epitome of a philosopher ("Socrates!" they crow, almost in unison, as they remember him

---

Philosophy and All of Us

A theory of philosophy is different from an ideology. While an ideology directs the actions and reactions of each individual regardless of whether she is aware of it, a philosophy is consciously thought out and presented to the world at large. Philosophy is academic, a defined way of finding meaning in life or searching for truth. Philosophy is:

- Clearly and carefully articulated
- Tested and evaluated through application to social or literary history
- The result of conscious consideration of personal and/or cultural ideology
- An investigation of the ultimate meaning (or lack of meaning) of life

Philosophy can be the work of an individual philosopher that has withstood rigorous examination by scholars. Few people have the time, resources, knowledge, or inclination to develop, test, and argue a method of philosophy. But learning about different philosophical theories can help us sort out our own take on the world around us and where we fit into the big picture.

Figure 6–2   Philosophy and All of Us

© 2006 by Lisa Schade Eckert from *How Does It Mean?* Portsmouth, NH: Heinemann.

from the movie *Bill and Ted's Excellent Adventure*). I explained the Socratic method—questioning until you either uncover truth or find there is no such thing as truth. I explained that philosophy considered sweeping questions, like What is reality? Who am I? What is truth? Does life have meaning? What is the difference between right and wrong? According to Socrates, the only true wisdom is in knowing that you know nothing.

"Geez, Matt," teased Jacob, "maybe you're smarter than you think!"

"Hey, Siddhartha would have liked Socrates," Danielle mused. "We should have talked about philosophy when we read that."

I also discussed Marxist philosophy. Even though we talked about his ideology, and categorized that under the designation of sociological criticism previously, I explained that he also posed philosophical questions about world history and the role of production and the labor of the "masses." Separating Marx's philosophy from his ideology was difficult for them (and for me), so we decided that it was acceptable to use a

Marxist approach in either a sociological or philosophical context. "But I think we'll wait to talk more about philosophy, if that's OK," I told them. "First you need to find a good book; we'll go from there."

Individual Novels

We started applying philosophical and sociological criticism by individually reading different novels that invite this particular approach. The novel is "the art form which raises questions about our existence in the world as self-conscious beings [exploring] human existence in the world" (Linn 1996, 74–75), making it an excellent vehicle for exploring philosophical thought. My purpose in developing the Novel Project (Figure 6–3) was not just to encourage students to read a good novel, but to help them learn about philosophical ideas, to identify the ways these ideas are depicted through the characters and events of the novel, and then to use those ideas to fill in gaps and construct meaning from the text. I devised this project also as practice for the final inquiry project, which I will detail in the next section, so students would have some experience and a starting point for their larger-group research.

The novel project was an individual one. I worked with the library media specialist to pull appropriate novels and bring them to my classroom on a cart, and I encouraged students to spend some time examining the books, eventually choosing the one that most interested them. Because this was World Literature, I chose predominantly novels written by authors from countries outside of the United States and Great Britain—or minority cultures from within—trying to represent as many nations as possible (see the appendix at the end of this book). The novels I put on the cart ranged from obviously philosophical works by Ayn Rand, Elie Wiesel, Gabriel García Márquez, Albert Camus, Jean-Paul Sartre, Chinua Achebe, and others, to more contemporary novels that still invited philosophical interpretation. I read an excerpt from *The Tao of Pooh* aloud to model a philosophical reading, and to show how it could be done with just about any book (I still have the Winnie the Pooh coffee mug one student gave me at the end of the year). I wanted the specific books I had chosen on a cart in my classroom, rather than just take my class to the library, because I wanted to give students the opportunity to talk about and compare novels, exploring them for at least two days before they had to make their final selection. Even after that time I allowed them to switch books during the first few days of library research if they felt the books were a little out of their league. Although I had made some careful choices in reading options (with help from the library media specialist), I didn't completely restrict them to the books we had put on the cart if they had a different idea or interest, but I did reserve the right to approve or nix any book they chose in the end. They had to

---

World Literature Novel Project
Authorial Philosophy/Ideology

For this project, you will be choosing one of the novels on the list you've been given. Your purpose is to explore the relationship between the author's life, sociohistoric relevance, and ideological views and the characters and events in the novel. The following areas must be exhaustively researched, learned, and shared by the time you finish your novel:

I. Author background

Research your author's philosophical or ideological views. Understand the message the author conveys throughout the story. You will be required to turn in author background research notes to ensure thorough research of appropriate materials in the library.

II. Ideological/philosophical base

Research the basic premise underlying the ideology/philosophy communicated in your novel. Know where it comes from and how it was utilized. Be able to use this knowledge to interpret specific aspects of your novel.

III. Time period

Research and understand the sociohistoric relevance of both the author's life and philosophy or ideology. Who else was practicing this method of understanding the world? Investigate the arts: visual artists, dramatic artists, other novelists. Who influenced the author? Look into the political climate of the time for influence as well.

IV. Annotated bibliography

Create a detailed bibliography of at least twenty sources. Each annotation should indicate the type of source, relevant sections of the source, and the value of the source. What can one learn from this material? Additional sources can translate into extra credit *if* they are relevant and useful.

V. Critical Response

Give a brief written response discussing your interpretation of the novel and the author's philosophy or ideology.

Figure 6–3   World Literature Novel Project: Authorial Philosophy/ Ideology

make a good case for an alternative choice; I tried to ensure that each student was reading something he hadn't read before and that it was substantive enough to fulfill the project requirements. But, because a thematic approach as I define it in this chapter is so universal, the issue of book choice can be based on any curricular goals. The books I included were simply the ones that were available to me from the school and local library.

The two class periods devoted to book choice were somewhat chaotic; there was a lot of movement as students passed books back and forth, asked questions, made comments about book covers, titles, and authors, vented frustration at wanting to read one that someone else had already chosen, and so on. Before students could identify a possible ideological or philosophical approach, or even begin to conceive of how to accomplish this, they had to read some of their novel. So on the third day I tried to reassure them. "Now we're just going to read for a while. Don't worry about anything else, and just get into the book. You can write down questions if you have them, mark the pages with sticky notes when you discover something interesting, maybe think about how you are making meaning happen, but mostly *read*. I can't even tell you exactly what to decide is important yet, but I will help you think about how to do that once you have a feel for the plot and characters. The most important thing right now is you and your relationship with the story." We spent three days in class just reading. If a student had a question, I would quietly and individually conference. If a student wanted to switch books after the first day I let them look the book cart over one more time, but after that they would have to revisit their choices after school or at lunch to avoid disrupting the class during reading time.

The next hurdle was for students to identify a main thematic concept that would serve as the basis for uncovering meaning in the story. We started with biographical research because it was familiar and would lead us to the tougher stuff about ideology and philosophy. We were following the pattern established in the previous unit on biographical criticism (biographical research as impetus for identifying theme), but this time we were digging in a little deeper by interrogating the underlying ideological and philosophical concepts. I wish I could say that I had carefully planned for all these details to fit together so nicely, but the progression just sort of happened as my students and I worked together to tackle these concepts. As we prepared to go to the library, I instructed them to explore the background of their particular author. I showed them some of the resources available in the reference section: *Dictionary of the History of Ideas*, the *Routledge Encyclopedia of Philosophy*, *Current Biography*, the *Dictionary of World Biography*, and, to their surprise, their World Literature textbook. "First, we'll work on a biographical approach, just like we did with Kafka. Who is the author as a person? What did the author believe? When did the author write? What do other people have to say about it? Use your textbook if the author is included. You already know how to do this, so you'll have a good start before we start thinking about your author's philosophy or ideology." I showed them again how to first look in the index of a source to find out if there was anything about their author because it was more detailed than the table of contents and they would save time. We spent a couple of days in the library researching authors before we began digging a little deeper. The library media specialist bookmarked some Internet sites from university English and philosophy departments that posted coursework on the subjects; the Internet Public Library (www.ipl.org) was very helpful, as well as the many other Internet resources students located with their search phrases. Online sources allowed students much more freedom to explore most of the approaches they chose. I made sure they knew they should be reading their books as homework, jotting down questions just like we did in class.

Even though we began by investigating the authors, simply assuming a biographical stance wasn't going to be enough to construct a thematic interpretation. I needed to provide the means for students to dig deeper into philosophical and ideological issues and really engage in a critical reading of the text. Once they felt like they knew a thing or two about the author I asked them to consider *why* the author wrote the story. What kind of worldview is represented? What do you learn about life and truth through the characters and events in the book? What larger questions or ideas could they identify? My only stipulation was that the concept they chose to focus on must be present in a legitimate source, like the ones I shared with them already, so they could zero in on the particulars of the philosophical or ideological school of thought they decided to investigate. Most were not familiar with the concepts of ideology and philosophy except for the brief introductions I had given, and felt uncomfortable at first. Once they were started, however, they became interested in the larger questions posed by these novels, and I found that I learned at least as much as they did. Several students chose philosophical methods I was not familiar with, but were included in the *Encyclopedia of Philosophy*, like Sufism (a branch of the Muslim faith). Even though the beginning phase of the project seemed hectic and time-consuming, the resulting discussion and exposure to philosophical thought and literature was well worth the stress of the beginning few days.

Some authors' ideological or philosophical views were more obvious than others. For example, Ayn Rand established the Objectivist movement, so it's a clear theme in her writing. There was even an Objectivist Club membership card in the paperback copy of *The Fountainhead* that

Dan was reading. Albert Camus' existentialist tendencies are well docu-
mented. But what about a book like Laura Esquivel's *Like Water for Choco-
late*, the novel Susan had chosen? She approached me in the library,
lamenting the lack of information beyond basic biographical and publication details. "Tell me about the story," I said. She told me about the magical recipes, the lovesick heroine, the overbearing mother. "What questions
do you have about the story itself?" I asked. She refers to her notes, reading some of her questions, including "How can food be magical? Why is
her mom so mean to her? Why can't she just marry the guy she loves?" I
asked her to consider the larger implications of these questions. Does
food represent love? How is love defined or portrayed in the story? Does
Tita have any power over her life? Is she oppressed by her mother or by
the society in which she lives? We talked about the narrative details that
might, in part, answer her questions. Susan considered Tita's powerlessness over her circumstances, then said, "Oh, yeah! Cooking is the only
thing that she can control in her life. It's the only power she has, because
that's what society expects from women. But her love also gives her
more power over her cooking." She was puzzled. "How do those things
go together? Which one is more important, power or love?" I told her
that it was up to her to decide as she continued reading. Essentially, she
recognized that she had two options: to focus on the philosophical question of the power of love, or the ideological issue of women in society.
Either of those themes would provide a "way in" to the story, set a purpose for her reading, and help her critically determine the meaning of
the story. This is not to say there aren't other concepts that are important
to the story, but the point is that she had identified two main concepts
and, rather than give up or become frustrated with a story that she just
couldn't understand, she could choose the details that meant something
to her based on her purpose for reading.

As students read and thought, I discovered that teaching novels in
this way promoted academic integrity. The research was difficult and they
had to put information into their own words to apply it to the various
novels they were reading, so they couldn't plagiarize by cutting and past-
ing from online sources (or copying from reference books). I had told
them to mark significant passages in their novels with sticky notes, and
their books were soon filled with them; this meant they really did have to
read. I also checked their reading by conducting mandatory individual
conferences during reading and library time; I noted these in the grade-
book. I told them it was OK to go out on a limb sometimes and they
should use everything they knew about strategies, reading, and stories to
make sense of the novel, even if they were a little nervous about doing so.

Because students had chosen their own path in this project, they
were very proud of their work and one by one, showed off to the class

what they learned by presenting a synopsis and review of the novel they chose. Most of them had found their way in to their novels, becoming even more aware of the reading and interpretive strategies they used. They used their prior knowledge, they predicted, analyzed, synthesized, and, finally, shared their meaning constructions with the class. For example, Marcus learned more about Brecht's "estrangement effect" and applied it to Douglas Adams' *The Hitchhiker's Guide to the Galaxy*; Amy presented an existentialist interpretation of *Things Fall Apart* by Chinua Achebe; and Dan, who had sent the card from his book into the Objectivist Club, shared the materials the organization sent to him when he presented *The Fountainhead*. As they shared their stories, they realized that becoming familiar with a particular philosophical approach meant they could apply it to many different texts, and they shared their thoughts with each other during the presentations. They also reported flexing their theoretical muscles at the family dinner table, in other classes, and during those awkward moments of a first date, using their fledgling knowledge as ammunition in discussion with unsuspecting peers, parents, and teachers (even with the principal, in one tense situation). They were ready to move on, and the novels served as a starting point for larger inquiry into these issues.

Thematic Criticism and Final Inquiry Project

By the time we had completed the Novel Project, there were only seven weeks left of school, and I wanted to give students further opportunity to expand on what they had already learned about literary theory and constructing meaning. I decided to end the year with a large project, although engaging students with thematic criticism does not require such an approach. My objective was also to see how much the students could do and how well they could independently research, as well as to provide the class with as much discussion of literature and theory as possible. To me, an extensive research project seemed like a good way to accomplish these goals. I gave students detailed guidelines and a specific schedule for the duration of the project (Figure 6–4).

This project required students to form small groups and research more fully one critical approach to literature that we had discussed so far as part of thematic criticism (existentialism, "others" in society, Marxist ideology, etc.), developing a detailed explication of literary examples from a specific geographic area or literary circle. Because this was World Literature, I asked them to choose topics and authors from outside the United States and Great Britain. "You can build on the ideas from one of the novels you've just finished, if that gets you started," I suggested. "Was there something you heard about that particularly interested you?

World Literature
Final Project/Presentation

For this project you will be working in groups of three or four and focusing on one major geographical or philosophical area. You will be researching both the social history and the literary tradition of the country or philosophical group, including any critical and philosophical theories and their effects on the literary output. Your final goal is to develop a forty-five-minute presentation incorporating the required information outlines below. We will be working for approximately five weeks in preparation for the presentation and I will require that you turn in materials during the process of research to check your progress.

Research Area Requirements for Successful Completion

I. Ideological and/or philosophical concept
    A. Discuss particular concepts important in the literary tradition of the area or group
        1. Existentialism?
        2. Religion?
        3. Marxism?
        4. Feminism?
    B. Identify an appropriate approach to the literature
    C. This section is worth 35 points

II. Social history relevant to literature
    A. Include here any significant governmental, historical, or social occurrences that are reflected in literature (in other words, briefly delve into an historical approach)
    B. 25 points

III. Major writers and their works
    A. Include at least one long novel or drama
        1. Present plot summary
        2. Discuss importance in literary tradition
        3. 20 points
    B. Analyze body of poetry including several poets significant to your focus area
        1. Explicate with copies for the class (turn in to me at least four days in advance if you need copies made)
        2. Utilize a defined critical approach
        3. 20 points
    C. Include short stories and essays you may discover
        1. Include copies for the class
        2. 20 points

continued

Figure 6–4   World Literature: Final Project/Presentation

IV. Outline to distribute to class
    A. Include an "agenda" of your presentation
    B. Define unfamiliar terms and ideas
    C. Give this to me four days in advance
    D. 20 points

V. Utilize visual aids
    A. Overheads, posters, maps, videos (short!), pictures, etc.
    B. 25 points

VI. Extras
    A. Music, food, costumes, props, etc. Create atmosphere!
    B. 20 points

VII. Annotated bibliography
    A. Include all materials used
    B. Differentiate between primary and secondary sources
    C. Use bibliography cards and MLA format
    D. 25 points

You will want to research constructively to define a specific focus for your presentation. Investigate philosophical methods, appropriate critical approaches, and progression of ideas relevant to your area of interest. BE PATIENT!! You will only identify this central focus after searching, reading, and generally exploring your chosen focus area.

Grading

This project will constitute your entire final marking-period grade. The final presentation is worth 200 points, however, you are not simply earning points on the actual day you present. You are earning points on all of the work required in preparation for it. Do not expect to be able to put this off until the night before and still pass; I am consciously working out point values to ensure group cooperation and participation throughout the next six weeks.

    Each group must designate individual responsibilities to all members. As a group you will keep a research log of your progress on a day-to-day basis, with each member recording his accomplishments or problems for the day. These journals will be kept in class so the entire group's work will be available every day even if someone is absent. I will be checking these journals to note your progress. Each student will receive an individual grade on journal entries! I reserve the right to deduct points from this portion of the assignment at my discretion based on your participation on any given day. If you are absent for any more than two days during the course of this project, you will lose three points per additional day.

Figure 6–4 *continued*

Or maybe you'd like to experiment with one of the theoretical approaches we learned about this year. Maybe you'd like to read some literature from a country or culture that interests you. The first thing you will need to do is decide within your group where you'd like to begin. There are written works from every country in the world, so you can't go wrong, although some will be easier to research than others. Look through your textbook for some ideas." Deciding on a group theme, or research focus, was, of course, the biggest hurdle. They could choose to focus on ideology, history, culture, society, or philosophy and locate poetry, essays, short stories, and one novel or full-length drama to read through their chosen lens. In order to accomplish this in a scope large enough to fulfill the requirements for the project but narrow enough to be realistic and manageable, students would have to draw upon a culture's literary tradition. I showed them the *Dictionary of World Biography* again, noting how it was divided by geographical region and listed influential novelists, thinkers, poets, and other artists in addition to historical and political figures from the country. This source gave students a quick glance at the intellectual developments of a given country, and led many of them to their final thematic focus. The World Literature textbook, of course, was also full of material from time periods and countries we hadn't covered and would also serve as an excellent starting point.

As with the novel project, for the first few days students were full of questions and concerns; I sat with each group and conferenced with them about their interests, questions and group responsibilities to help them begin to consider their options. They had to negotiate with group members to decide on a basic idea, and evaluate that idea to see if it was a viable basis for research. Once they had decided on a country or cultural base and some options for reading material, we set about finding sometimes obscure novels, short stories, drama, and poetry. The library media specialist helped locate materials in the library, and I organized a trip to the local university library to let them browse there for sources and literature that would have been hard to find otherwise. I used my library card to check out necessary materials, and kept them in the classroom (unless a student who really needed to read one overnight vowed in blood to bring it back the next day). Each member was not required to read each individual literary work, so we didn't need multiple copies; instead they assigned roles to one another, dividing the reading responsibilities however they chose. But I did want them to discuss what they read within the larger context of theory and put it all together into a presentation for the rest of the class. In order to do this, they had to think and talk about theory, literature, and research strategies, and brainstorm ideas for ways of presenting what they eventually discovered. This is why I had introduced students to sociological and philosophical theory in the first place; these critical approaches were broad enough to apply to any cultural literature, but still provided scaffolding to help students find meaning in what they read. Their research and reading would culminate in a forty-five-minute presentation centering on their chosen country and literary tradition or the development of a particularly influential literary circle.

Completing the project required students to draw upon all the critical and research skills they had learned throughout the year, and become more independent thinkers and learners, but I was sure to make my expectations very clear. Modes of inquiry were completely student generated, yet I established specific requirements and due dates to monitor student progress and keep them on track. The tightly organized schedule was crucial for ensuring that students were on task and for providing them with enough feedback so they did not become overwhelmed or lost. I created a schedule grid with students (with pen and paper in class while we were discussing the end of the year) and made copies for each group (Figure 6–5), and I checked off due dates and materials they turned in as the weeks went past. Students could check their progress at any time, and continually plan their next step.

The project also ensured flexibility for students and for me as we proceeded one day at a time. My role was that of facilitator; I taught minilessons to individual groups and the class as a whole, reviewing concepts of theory, research, and interpretation. I conferenced with each group on a daily basis, and did not even bring the entire class together; often students just went straight to work when class began without any direction from me. I designed the particular details of the project to ensure that students did not procrastinate and set due dates intermittently so they had time to think of the big picture, but also had to pay attention to the small steps along the way (Figure 6–5). Students were required to turn in research questions, bibliography cards, note cards, and an annotated bibliography. I also required them to keep a journal detailing their progress, and asked them to write at the end of every class about what they had accomplished individually and as a group, their questions, and their discoveries. The journal proved to be invaluable, as many students kept all their research materials in it, and used it to keep track of and develop ideas. But the journal also helped keep me informed about each group's progress, and if there was a problem that students were not comfortable sharing with me in a group setting, they could write it there. For example, if one group had a member who wasn't pulling her weight, the others could write about their concern in their journals and I could deal with the problem without having a student risk "telling" on the offending group member. Unless a certain group and I agreed otherwise, the final grade would be a group grade, so this aspect of the journal became an important way to monitor group interaction.

*WORLD LIT PROJECT SCHEDULE

MONDAY	TUESDAY	WEDNESDAY	THURSDAY	FRIDAY
APRIL 19 LOOK AT SCHEDULE: COMPLAIN!!	20 LIBRARY	21	NOVELS 22 IDENTIFIED We must find them!	BIB CARDS 23 DUE!
26 Reading DAY	27 FINDER SHEETS DUE!!	28 WALDO LIBRARY!!	29 JOURNAL ARTICLES DUE!! READ!	30 STATEMENT OF FOCUS DUE!! READ!
MAY 3 DISCUSS PROM ATTIRE (Briefly!) READ! AV Class Begins	4 READ!	5 READ! Class	6 READ!	7 Any printing yet? READ!
10 READ! class	11 HANDOUTS FOR PRINTING should start rolling in — Keep Ms. Schade organized!	12 NOTECARDS DUE!! (25) class	13 ANNOTATED BIBLIOGRAPHY DUE!	14 PRESENTATION #1
17 PRESENTATION #2!! MOVIES? FOOD? FUN? Class	18 PRESENTATION #3!! BOOKS? DRAMA? FUN?	19 PRESENTATION #4!! PHILOSOPHY? LANGUAGE? FUN! Class	20 #5!! HISTORY? RELIGION? FUN!	21 #6!! POLITICS? CRITICISM? FUN?
24 #7!! MUSIC? ART? Class FUN!	25 #8!! SHORT STORIES? POETRY? FUN!	26 REVIEW! class	27 EXAM! YOU'RE DONE!!! IF YOU PASS↓	BEACH!!!

Figure 6–5   World Literature Project Schedule

I didn't see any rehearsals of their final presentations, so I didn't know exactly what would happen on these days. I relied on what I had learned during the group conferences and on my faith in these students as learners. I had handed them a certain amount of autonomy and responsibility and, by doing so, had communicated my confidence in their knowledge and unique strengths. I felt this was an important aspect of not only the entire year of World Literature, but particularly this project. During each presentation, the rest of the class wrote comments for the group and posed a couple of questions that I would later use for the final exam (I was required to give one); they turned these in to me at the end of the hour. I think it is important here to note again that these were not advanced students, that many of these students had not successfully completed a literature-based high school English class. Any discrepancies or inconsistencies in their research as I describe it here is still present because I want to show the results of this project exactly as the students shared it with me and the class. I have chosen just a sample of the projects completed in World Literature, and have had a difficult time choosing which to highlight. Each one reflected the strengths, interests, and sometimes cultural background of the students who prepared it, so they were all very unique. I still feel so proud of these students as I write this, and am so thankful for what they taught me about being a teacher and a student.

Presentation Days

I walked into my classroom on the morning of the first presentation to find that Mary, Shawn, and Eli had already been there for some time, preparing their "environment." They had convinced the custodian to let them in early, and transformed the room into a Brazilian rain forest. They lugged in palm trees, stuffed animals, and yards of plastic vines to create the environment, complete with a hut they made out of a giant sheet of brown paper, suspended from the ceiling with paper clips and decorated with more vines and flowers. They had cut out a door and stored all props and accessories behind the paper hut, so during the presentation they came in and out of it at various intervals. They spent the last few minutes before class running around to complete finishing touches while I went to retrieve the VCR unit. They were planning to show a short film describing the horrors of life for homeless children in Brazilian cities as a part of their emphasis on the disparity in Brazilian societal structure. After quickly changing into their costumes, the group distributed their handout, entitled "Feminist/Marxist Literature in Brazil," to the class. Their central thesis was "Social Realism: Contemporary Brazilian authors openly examined the social ills of their time in order to expose people to them and to eventually facilitate change." They had chosen this particular topic at the request of one group member. She spoke Spanish at home, but had a relative who had been to Brazil and learned some Portuguese (the language spoken in Brazil) and she had become interested in both the country and the language. They shared details from *I Would Have Loved Him if I Had Not Killed Him*, by Edgard Telles Ribeiro, an obscure novel they had discovered during their research and located at the university library; the short story "The Secret Heart" by Joaquim Maria Machado de Assis; and poetry, including "Vigil," by Cecilia Meireles and "Cemetery in Pernambuco," by Joao Cabral de Melo Neto. Central issues for this group were the plight of homeless children, who had little hope of living until the age of the students in this World Literature classroom, and the oppression of women in Brazilian society.

The group presenting the next day, Kristi, Dan, and Melanie, had focused on the *Tao te Ching* and its influence in the Chinese literary tradition and on contemporary works as well. They hung strings of paper lanterns, lit incense, set up a small bubbling fountain, and played soft Chinese music throughout their presentation. They began by silently walking in slow circles, allowing the class to absorb the ambiance they had created, to illustrate the meditative search for "the way" and the concept that the journey is more important than the destination. In their presentation, they included excerpts of the *Tao te Ching*, the *Chinese Book of Changes*, and *The Tao of Pooh* (even though I had read some excerpts, this was central to what they wanted to accomplish so I didn't mind), among other works, to exemplify the tradition of Taoist philosophy. The Russian group, Amy, Ashley, Jacob, and Anna, introduced us to "acmeism" as described by Russian poet Anna Akhmatova and her literary circle. "The 'acme' of something is the highest point, the best you can get," explained Ashley. "To reach the acme is to write a poem or story that perfectly describes a situation or emotion without using extra words or images; that's what they were trying to do." Their discussion of acmeism included references to Tolstoy's *Anna Karenina* (which, they argued, reached the acme as a novel "even if there are a *lot* of words in it," according to Jacob), "The Man in the Case," by Anton Chekov, and the poems "Requiem" and "Evening," by Anna Akhmatova. Actually, I fell in love with Akhmatova's poetry after these students introduced it to me and still enjoy reading her work.

Danielle, Tom, and Susan focused on the topic of French existentialism. Instead of putting up elaborate decorations, they spent a great deal of time taking everything down. Posters, bulletin boards, signs, and student work that had covered my walls for the year were, to these existentialists, "meaningless and in the way." They wanted nothing significant to be visible; they even covered the clock with blank white paper (causing much anxiety among their classmates, but certainly emphasizing how dependent we were on something as meaningless as time). While some groups had elaborately prepared food for their presentations, this group handed out water and crackers. Susan began: "I glance around the room and a violent disgust floods me. What am I doing here? Why are these people here? Why are they eating? It's true they don't know they exist." This excerpt from Jean-Paul Sartre's *The Wall* introduced their discussion of the existentialist reduction of life to a series of "meaningless non-events." Poetry included "The Man Alone," by Aragon, and "Atheist Prayer," by Pierre Emmanuel. (I worried that this might offend some students, but no one objected.) They invoked Sartre again: "To do something is to create existence—and there's quite enough as it is."

Students immediately latched on to this. "Hey! I like this guy! We don't have to do anything . . . let's just go now!" laughed Ryan.

Susan glared at him. "You don't get it. He said there was enough existence as it is, but he was putting more things into existence himself. When he wrote that, he put it into existence! So you can't believe him, because he doesn't follow his own advice."

This generated a discussion about existentialism and nihilism, which evolved directly into a discussion of the literary theory of deconstruction. "Is there really existentialist criticism?" Jacob asked. "How can books mean nothing?"

"Maybe they're just like Socrates" mused Melanie. We looked at her, puzzled. "You know, question everything until you know it. If you keep asking questions, pretty soon you're not sure what you know!"

Ray Linn, in *A Teacher's Introduction to Postmodernism* (1996) addresses the troubling nature of this textual approach: "The postmodern idea that there is no truth might at first seem demoralizing . . . but it is also liberating. Not only are we liberated from the burden of searching for what cannot be found, we are also liberated from an oppressive urge to shove others and ourselves into preconceived cages . . . [this liberation] redirects our energies toward what human beings are good at—creating ourselves and the worlds we live in" (145). My students never found it depressing. They were just curious, which I believe is because it was the students themselves who discovered deconstruction within their own critical discourse; I did not introduce or require them to explore it as an interpretive approach. Susan had seen right through Sartre's argument. She did not have to accept my interpretation of it as something she would have to know or apply for a grade, and the rest of the class followed her lead. We talked about the experience of the war in Europe and the effect it must have had on the way people felt about life and society. Patrick, who was in the Holocaust group that had also centered on existentialism, said, "But it does mean something when they write about it.

It means something when I read it, anyway. Isn't that the point? Maybe somebody could come in here and say that the books we read don't make sense, but they do to *me*."

Students were liberated as they became more confident in their interpretive abilities, and could question some of the most basic premises of postmodern theory, while accepting the relevance of others. They were also creating worlds from the books that they had read and developing confidence in themselves. Patrick, in saying that books meant something to him, was referring to the creative act of constructing meaning from text—a critical, aesthetic reading, in which he "listened to himself" (Rosenblatt 1994, 25). I sat in the classroom that day and was amazed at the way these students dealt with the deepest reaches of theory, both in life and literature.

Literature of the Holocaust

The final presentation day arrived, and John, Patrick, Ryan, and Matt strung red lights around the room in random circles. The lights symbolized, and in fact closely resembled, the barbed wire surrounding World War II Nazi concentration camps. They covered the windows with black paper, readied a spotlight to shine on them as they presented their theme: "Eastern European Literature and the Holocaust" (Figure 6–6). Patrick, who was very thin and wiry, was dressed almost too convincingly as a camp inmate, in long underwear with black duct tape creating the stripes that clearly identified Jewish prisoners. "Nobody really wrote anything for about *ten years* after the Jews were liberated," marveled John (ten years is an awfully long time to a sixteen-year-old). "The subject was completely avoided. Do you know why? Because people needed ten years to recover from the war. They tried to find meaning for what they lived through. But how can there be any meaning for that? People really began to write about it in the 1960s because the move toward self-expression for everyone made the time right for publishing their stories. Even then, nobody could find the meaning for wasting six million lives." Matt added, "Elie Wiesel was really the first to write a lot that many people read. He paved the way for people to write about their experiences. He also looked for a meaning in what happened to him, but couldn't find any. In the book *Night* he said, 'Never shall I forget that night . . . which has turned my life into one long night . . . Never shall I forget that nocturnal silence which deprived me, for all eternity, of the desire to live.' Eyewitness accounts like his were the first things to appear [in print] because people wrote about it so they could try and understand it." They discuss *The House on Prague Street* by Hans Demetz, poetry by

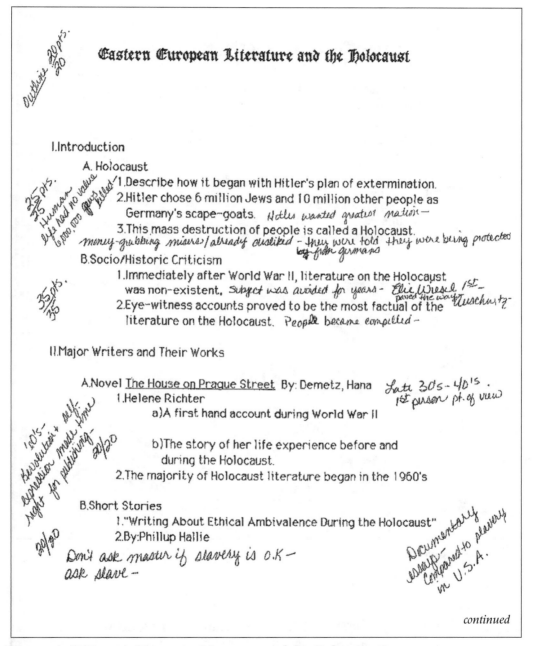

Eastern European Literature and the Holocaust

Outline 20 pts. 20

I.Introduction

   A. Holocaust

25 pts. 25 Human left had no value 6,000,000 people killed

      1.Describe how it began with Hitler's plan of extermination.

      2.Hitler chose 6 million Jews and 10 million other people as
         Germany's scape-goats. *Hitler wanted greatest nation—*

      3.This mass destruction of people is called a Holocaust. *money-grubbing misers / already disliked – they were told they were being protected by from germans*

   B.Socio/Historic Criticism

35 pts. 35

      1.Immediately after World War II, literature on the Holocaust
         was non-existent. *Subject was avoided for years – Elie Wiesel 1st – paved the way Auschwitz–*

      2.Eye-witness accounts proved to be the most factual of the
         literature on the Holocaust. *People became compelled –*

II.Major Writers and Their Works

   A.Novel <u>The House on Prague Street</u> By: Demetz, Hana *Late 30's-40's. 1st person pt. of view*

      1.Helene Richter

         a)A first hand account during World War II

'80's – Revolution & self-expression made time right for publishing – 20/20

         b)The story of her life experience before and
            during the Holocaust.

      2.The majority of Holocaust literature began in the 1960's

   B.Short Stories

20/20

      1."Writing About Ethical Ambivalence During the Holocaust"

      2.By:Phillup Hallie

Don't ask master if slavery is O.K – ask slave –

Documentary essay – compared to slavery in U.S.A.

continued

Figure 6–6 Eastern European Literature and the Holocaust

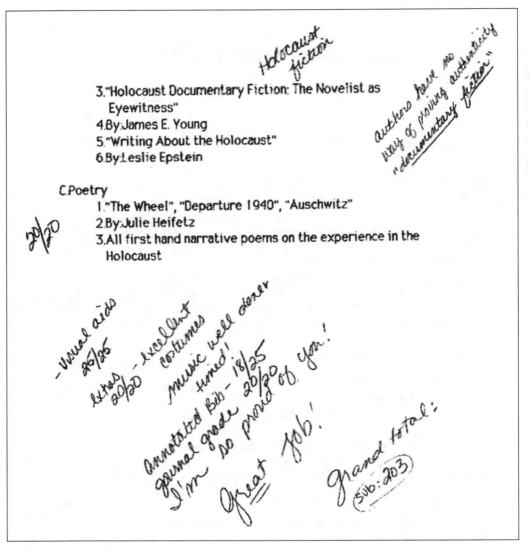

3. "Holocaust Documentary Fiction: The Novelist as
   Eyewitness"
4. By: James E. Young
5. "Writing About the Holocaust"
6. By: Leslie Epstein

C. Poetry

1. "The Wheel", "Departure 1940", "Auschwitz"
2. By: Julie Heifetz
3. All first hand narrative poems on the experience in the
   Holocaust

Figure 6–6   continued

Julie Heifetz ("The Wheel," "Departure," and "Auschwitz") as well as several critical essays regarding literature of the Holocaust. They were so proud to have discovered a new literary genre: "documentary fiction." In their reading, they found the Holocaust "was compared to slavery in the United States. That makes it seem closer to home. Every society persecutes one group or another. If you want the real picture, don't ask the master if slavery is OK, ask the slave."

I was particularly proud of this group because they had always had difficulty with reading, literature, and constructing meaning. All four of them had been in my class before and we had gone round and round about the "gray areas" of finding meaning in literature. Learning with them throughout the year, watching them first realize they could engage in constructing literary meaning independently and then become fascinated with the material they were reading, was enormously gratifying. They told me afterward that knowing about philosophy and theory had made literary interpretation comprehensible. They found it made sense to understand literature through a philosophical stance, to thematically explore literary representations that exemplify the meaningless Nazi persecution of Jewish people. How is it possible to understand the wasting of so many lives?

Obviously students could stretch and grow through their own inquiry. I couldn't have designed better learning activities for students than these presentations, as well as the presentations of the Japanese group, who focused on a sociological reading of *Black Rain* by Masuji Ibuse; or the South African group, who read *Cry the Beloved Country*, by Alan Paton; short stories "The Leopard Woman," by Roger D. Adams, and "The Black Dress," by Danielle Millan; poems "Lullaby," by Jacob Cronin, and "Small Passing," by Ingrid de Kok, and showed an excerpt of the film *The Power of One*. The group that presented on New Zealand's literary history focused on the uniqueness of the island nation (including the natural world), Maori oral tradition and personal memoirs of pioneers. They read the novel *Spinster*, by Sylvia Ashton-Warner; the short story "Insulation," by Janet Frame; poetry by Allen Curnow and Eli Ireland; a selection of Maori folktales, and, finally, shared a video of the beauty of the country.

The End, or Another Beginning?

After finishing their final exam, students danced out of the room to join the throng in the halls heading for summer vacation. I stood at the door, waving and exchanging hugs and a few tears with those seniors who were suddenly nostalgic about their high school years (two days ago they were "so over this school"). I was back at my desk, surveying the aftermath and just beginning to reflect on the events of the past year when the English department chair poked her head in the door.

"You survived," she smiled. She walked in and handed me a couple of book catalogues. "Good, then you can take a look at these and pick out some books for next year. You've got more money to spend now, so go ahead and order several classroom sets. Can you give me an order before you leave for the summer?"

"What, did someone will us money? Why do I have more money to spend on books?" I had already spent the small amount budgeted for books next year to build on my classroom library.

"Enrollment numbers are finally done. Get ready, because you have three sections of World Literature next year. That entitles you to more money." She walked out the door to finish her rounds, saying, "We're going to have to order fifty new textbooks, too."

I knew the numbers were going to be higher next year, but not that high. I quickly finished grading final exams so I could consider books I might order, several of which would be those found by my students in their research this year. I reached for my plan book, contemplating another summer spent tweaking goals and units for three sections of World Literature next year.

Further Teaching Suggestions

- The Individual Novel project could also be effectively organized as small-group, literature-circle readings of assigned novels. While this limits choice and reading opportunities for students, it moves along a bit more quickly than individual reading/presenting.

- To model a philosophical reading (interpretation), show an episode of *The Simpsons* and share the introduction and a couple of chapters from *The Simpsons and Philosophy: The D'oh! of Homer*, by William Irvin, Mark T. Conrad, and Aeon J. Skoble (2001, Chicago, IL: Open Court). The book is accessible, funny, and addresses specific philosophical concepts.

- Individual and group conferencing is crucial throughout. Make time to sit and talk with students about their reading and progress.

More Readings for Teaching Thematic Theory (see the appendix for more suggestions)

After the First Death by Robert Cormier

Gone with the Wind by Margaret Mitchell

The Lives and Loves of a She-Devil by Faye Weldon

Parrot in the Oven by Victor Martinez

Appendix
Novel List for Individual Novel Project

Author	Title
Achebe, Chinua	*Things Fall Apart*
Anaya, Rudolfo	*Bless Me, Ultima*
Atwood, Margaret	*The Handmaid's Tale*
Böll, Heinrich	*The Lost Honor of Katharina Blum*
Camus, Albert	*The Fall*
Camus, Albert	*The Stranger*
Conrad, Joseph	*Heart of Darkness*
Conrad, Joseph	*Lord Jim*
Emecheta, Buchi	*The Bride Price*
Esquivel, Laura	*Like Water for Chocolate*
Gordimer, Nadine	*July's People*
Hesse, Hermann	*Steppenwolf*
Hesse, Hermann	*Demian*
Kazantzakis, Nikos	*Zorba the Greek*
Kazantzakis, Nikos	*The Last Temptation of Christ*
Kingston, Maxine Hong	*The Woman Warrior*
Lord, Bette Bao	*Spring Moon*
Mann, Thomas	*Buddenbrooks*
Markandaya, Kamala	*Handful of Rice*
Markandaya, Kamala	*Nectar in a Sieve*
Márquez, Gabriel García	*One Hundred Years of Solitude*
Mishima, Yukio	*The Sound of Waves*
Paton, Alan	*Cry the Beloved Country*
Rand, Ayn	*Atlas Shrugged*
Rand, Ayn	*The Fountainhead*
Remarque, Erich Maria	*All Quiet on the Western Front*
Remarque, Erich Maria	*The Road Back*
Saint-Exupéry, Antoine de	*Wind, Sand, and Stars*

Author	Title
Sartre, Jean-Paul	*Nausea*
Sartre, Jean-Paul	*No Exit*
Solzhenitsyn, Aleksandr	*One Day in the Life of Ivan Denisov*
Solzhenitsyn, Aleksandr	*Cancer Ward*
Tan, Amy	*The Joy Luck Club*
Tan, Amy	*The Kitchen God's Wife*
Wiesel, Elie	*Dawn*
Wiesel, Elie	*Night*

References

Abrams, M. H. 1988. *A Glossary of Literary Terms*. Chicago: Holt, Rinehart and Winston.

Albert, Susan Wittig, Richard Cohen, Rose Sallberg Kam, David Adams Leeming, Thomas Monsell, Carroll Moulton, Susanna Nied, and Eileen Hillary Oshinsky.1993. *World Literature*. Chicago: Holt, Rinehart and Winston.

Barthes, Roland. 2001. "The Death of the Author." In *The Norton Anthology of Theory and Criticism*. Edited by Vincent B. Leitch, pp. 1466–70. New York: W.W. Norton.

Brewer, Linda. 1996. "20/20." In *Microfiction: An Anthology of Really Short Stories*. Edited by Jerome Stern, pp. 34–35. New York: W.W. Norton.

Campbell, Joseph. 1988. "The Hero's Adventure." *Power of Myth: Episode I.* With Bill Moyers. Montauk, NY: PBS Mystic Fire Productions.

Campbell, Joseph. 1968. *The Hero with a Thousand Faces*. Princeton, NJ: Princeton University.

Craig, Edward, ed. 1988. *Encyclopedia of Philosophy*. Vol 1–10. New York: Routledge.

Culler, Jonathan. 1975. *Structuralist Poetics: Structuralism, Linguistics and the Study of Literature*. New York: Cornell University Press.

Eagleton, Terry. 1996. *Literary Theory: An Introduction*. Minneapolis: University of Minnesota Press.

Eliot, Alexander. 1976. *The Universal Myths: Heroes, Gods, Tricksters and Others*. New York: Meridian.

Ferry, David. 1992. *Gilgamesh*. New York: The Noonday Press.

Fish, Stanley. 1999. *The Stanley Fish Reader*. Edited by H. Aram Veeser. Malden, MA: Blackwell Publishers.

Frisch, Shelley. Trans. 2005. *The Decisive Years*. New York: Harcourt.

Frye, Northrop. 2001. "The Archetypes of Literature." In *The Norton Anthology of Theory and Criticism*. Edited by Vincent B. Leitch, pp. 1445–57. New York: W.W. Norton.

Gardner, John, and John Maier. 1984. *Gilgamesh*. New York: Vintage Books.

Graff, Gerald. 2000. "Disliking Books at an Early Age." In *Falling into Theory: Conflicting Views on Reading Literature*, pp. 40–48. New York: Bedford/St. Martin Press.

Hesse, Hermann. 1982. *Siddhartha*. Trans. Hilda Rosner. New York: Bantam Classics.

Hirsch, E. D., Jr. 1987. "Objective Interpretation." In *Contexts for Criticism*. Edited by Donald Keesey, pp. 26–38. Mountain View, CA: Mayfield.

Iser, Wolfgang. 2000. *The Range of Interpretation*. New York: Columbia University Press.

Jung, Carl G. 1976. *The Symbolic Life: Miscellaneous Writings*. Trans. R. F. C. Hull. Princeton NJ: Princeton University Press.

Kafka. 1991. Produced and directed by Stephen Soderburgh. Hollywood, CA: Paramount Studios. Videocassette.

Kafka, Franz. 1974. "Letter to His Father." In *I Am a Memory Come Alive*, edited by Nahum Glatzer. New York: Schocken Books.

Keesey, Donald, ed. 1987. *Contexts for Criticism*. Mountain View, CA: Mayfield.

Kermode, Frank. 1987. "What Precisely Are the Facts?" In *Contexts for Criticism*. Edited by Donald Keesey, pp. 287–92. Mountain View, CA: Mayfield.

Levi, Jan Heller, ed. 1995. *A Muriel Rukeyser Reader*. New York: W. W. Norton.

Linn, Ray. 1996. *A Teacher's Introduction to Postmodernism*. Urbana, IL: National Council of Teachers of English.

Magill, Frank N., and John Roth, eds. 1990. *Masterpieces of World Philosophy*. New York: HarperCollins.

Magill, Frank N. and Christina Moose, eds. 2000. *Dictionary of World Biography*. Pasadena, CA: Salem Press.

McCormick, Kathleen. 1996. "Reading Lessons and Then Some: Toward Developing Dialogues between Critical Theory and Reading Theory." In *Critical Theory and the Teaching of Literature*. Edited by James F. Slevin. Urbana, IL: NCTE.

Mistral, Gabriela. 1992. "Why Reeds Are Hollow." Trans. William Jay Smith. *Literary Cavalcade* (January): 3–5.

Myers, D. G. 1994. "On the Teaching of Literary Theory." *Philosophy and Literature* 18 (January): 326–36.

Obbink, Laura Apol. 1992. "Feminist Theory in the Classroom: Choices, Questions, Voices." *English Journal* 81(7): 38–43.

Philion, Thomas. 2001. "'Is It Too Late to Get a Program Change?': The Role of Oppositionality in Secondary English Education." *English Education* 34(1): 50–70.

Read, Herbert, Michael Fordham and Gerhard Adler, eds. 1953–78. *Collected Works of C. G. Jung*. 20 Volumes. London: Routledge. (Quotations in this book are identified by volume and paragraph number.)

Return of the Jedi. 1983. Produced and directed by George Lucas. Los Angeles, Ca: Twentieth Century Fox Film Corporation.

Riazanov, David. 1996. *Karl Marx and Frederick Engels: An Introduction to Their Lives*. Online text. Marxists Internet Archive (www.marxists.org). http://www.marxists.org/archive/riazanov/works/1927-ma/ch03.htm. Last accessed April 7, 2006. Originally published in 1937. New York: Monthly Review Press.

Rosenblatt, Louise M. 1994. *The Reader, the Text, the Poem: The Transactional Theory of the Literary Work*. Carbondale, IL: Southern Illinois University Press.

Ryan, Michael. 1999. *Literary Theory: A Practical Introduction*. Malden, MA: Blackwell Publishers.

Sloan, Glenna Davis. 1991. *The Child as Critic: Teaching Literature in Elementary and Middle Schools*. New York: Teachers College Press, Columbia University.

Smith, Frank. 1997. *Reading Without Nonsense*. New York: Teachers College Press, Columbia University.

Spendler, Dale. 1982. *Women of Ideas and What Men Have Done to Them: From Aphra Behn to Adrienne Rich*. London: Routledge Press.

Stafford, William. 1998. "Fifteen." In *The Way It Is: New and Selected Poems,* p. 106. St. Paul, MN: Graywolf Press.

Star Wars. 1977. Produced and directed by George Lucas. Los Angeles, CA: Twentieth Century Fox Film Corporation.

Stevens, Anthony. 1994. *Jung.* Oxford University Press.

Tolkien, J. R. R. 1966. *The Hobbit.* Boston: Houghton.

Wiener, Philip P. *Dictionary of the History of Ideas.* 1980. Macmillan.

Wilhelm, Jeffrey D. 1997. *You Gotta BE the Book: Teaching Engaged and Reflective Reading with Adolescents.* New York: Teachers College Press, Columbia University; Urbana, IL: NCTE.

Williams, Raymond. 1977. *Marxism and Literature.* Oxford, U.K.: Oxford University Press.

Index